Rethinking Enterprise Software Risk:
Controlling the Main Risk Factors on IT Projects

Shaun Snapp

Rethinking Enterprise Software Risk: Controlling the Main Risk Factors on IT Projects

For information about this title or to order other books and/or electronic media, contact the publisher:
SCM Focus Press
PO Box 29502 #9059
Las Vegas, NV 89126-9502
http://www.scmfocus.com/scmfocuspress
(408) 657-0249

ISBN: 978-1-939731-30-2

Printed in the United States of America

Cover and interior design by: 1106 Design

Contents

CHAPTER 1

Introduction

It should go without saying that implementation success and time-lines are probabilistic. Generally enterprise software is complex and dependent upon a number of factors, including the software itself. Furthermore, it is well known—at least among executive decision makers—that software implementation is risky business. So why do so many companies behave as if project success is a certainty?

How do we know that success is assumed to be a given? Well, project and software selection, as traditionally practiced, rely upon the assumption that the implementation will be successful, and that the probability of success is **equal among all applications** under consideration. However, undertaking a project or software selection without approximating the project's risk is a poor way to make decisions about either projects or software. Although it goes against common sense, most companies do not estimate a project's probability of success prior to deciding which project to fund. Instead, they make the naive assumption that all projects will succeed, even though on average IT projects are considered a success only 50 percent of the time, and can be quantitatively shown to have a positive return about 35 percent of the time. (In a few paragraphs we will discuss the math behind these values; these statistics involve much more detail and complexity than is generally understood.)

There is little doubt that a high percentage of IT implementations fail. In fact, as an IT consultant I have observed that the failure rate is higher than published. The reason is rarely discussed; it is because all success and failure estimations rely upon self-reporting—that is, it's assumed that the company itself knows if the implementation was a success or failure. Often implementing companies do not know (and most do not spend the time to measure) if an implementation was a success; therefore only the most obvious measurements tend to be used, as explained in the following quotations:

> *"In addition Bradford and Sandy (2002) reported that 57 percent of the companies they interviewed had not attempted to assess the performance of their ERP systems owing to a lack of empirically effective evaluation models.*
>
> *According to Parr and Shanks (2000) 'ERP project success simply means bringing the project in on time and on budget.' So, most ERP projects start with a basic management drive to target faster*

implementation and a more cost-effective project… Summarizing, the project may seem successful if the time/budget constraints have been met, but the system may still be an overall failure or vice versa. So these conventional measures of project success are only partial and possibly misleading measures when taken in isolation (Shenhar and Levy, 1997)."

— Measures of Success in Project Implementing
Enterprise Resource Planning

Obvious measurements should include whether or not a system becomes operational, or if the system makes it impossible to send out invoices, or otherwise causes a loss to the business. However, a system can be operational and seem to work, yet provides poor quality output or requires constant manual adjustment. One can implement a new system that utilizes a complex set of methods, but because either the software was poorly designed or was improperly implemented, the quality of the output can be the same or even worse than the system it replaced. When this happens, there is a strong tendency to declare the system "successful" in any case. The business users may complain—and IT may respond that the system is working properly but the users don't know how to use it. Sometimes IT will bring in an expert to review the system, but what they really want is the system blessed. I know; I am one of those experts who is called in, and frequently I have found that when users complain about system output, typically they are correct. Any way you want to look at it, enterprise software implementation is a risky business.

There are several different approaches to managing project risk. Some common approaches (which don't work) involve seeking assurance from outside the company; these are the topic of Chapter 2: "Enterprise Software Risk Management Misconceptions." For years I have told stories of the easily avoidable errors—both in SCM Focus articles and to friends and family. When you talk to people within the industry, often a creeping cynicism—a *"well, that's the way it is"* mentality—comes into the discussion. However, outsiders who are not yet numb to poor management and uninformed decision-making are typically shocked. IT implementations very much have a degree of repetitiveness to their errors.

Books and Other Publications on Managing IT Project Risk

I perform a comprehensive literature review before I begin writing any book. One of my favorite research quotations is from the highly respected RAND Corporation, a think tank based in sunny Santa Monica, California—a location not far from where I grew up and where I used to walk with my friend when I was in high school—at that time having no idea of the historically significant institution that I used to walk by on my lost surfing weekends. RAND's *Standards for High Quality Research and Analysis* publication makes the following statement regarding how its research references other work.

> "A high-quality study cannot be done in intellectual isolation: It
> necessarily builds on and contributes to a body of research and
> analysis. The relationships between a given study and its predecessors
> should be rich and explicit. The study team's understanding of
> past research should be evident in many aspects of its work, from
> the way in which the problem is formulated and approached to the
> discussion of the findings and their implications. The team should
> take particular care to explain the ways in which its study agrees,
> disagrees, or otherwise differs importantly from previous studies.
> Failure to demonstrate an understanding of previous research lowers
> the perceived quality of a study, despite any other good characteristics
> it may possess."

Many books have been published on **project risk management**. This is the first book that I have written where so many books were available already; often I will write a book that turns out to be the only book on the topic. After reviewing these books on project risk management, I could find only two about software implementation or IT risk management. The other books were on managing the risk on any type of project. Authors with the PMP project management certification wrote many of the books—that is, they are professional project managers. While I managed projects for several years in the late 1990s, it was an interesting diversion and not what I have done for most of my career. I am a technologist. Thus, this book is written from a very different perspective than any of the books on risk management. It is also different from the two books about software project risk management in that the book does not focus on specific tactics, but rather on an approach to managing the information that is promoted by the entities that work in the enterprise software space. While many of the risk management books are dedicated to risk management matrixes and the calculation of probabilities for various risky alternatives, this book will not include any of that. That is not my expertise. My expertise lies in technology and how the organizations that provide software, services and advice on projects operate.

The type and quality of information provided by various entities is a touchy subject because, as I point out in this book, usually this information is intended more to improve the condition of the information provider than the receiver. Not many authors are interested in courting controversy, and this is why I believe no book like this has yet been written. Certainly, other books that describe different dimensions of the problem of risk management are also good to read. However, managing a project's risk is about more than the tactical elements of how to estimate risk. All of the material that I reviewed for this book had something to offer, but seemed to miss a major component of risk: the quality (or lack of quality) of the advice provided to companies. In fact, this component is missed in all of the writings on the topic of enterprise software risk that I could find. Implementing companies do not make enterprise software decisions alone; they rely heavily on advisors, and generally these advisors are considered to be the experts in all areas related to enterprise software implementation. Most authors will not address this issue as they don't like controversy, and the advisors happen to be very influential and prestigious.

Reducing the risk of software implementations and increasing the probability of success means doing some nonconformist thinking. I provide all the information in this book; as the reader all you have to do is consider the logic of what I have written and be open to the message. If you do that, you will be far ahead of your counterparts who are not open to different thinking and are simply following the consensus viewpoint. The consensus viewpoint is conformist, and furthermore is not doing the implementation of enterprise software any favors. In fact, the entities from which you will receive information in the enterprise software space rely upon the fact that you will think in a conformist manner, and this allows them to control your thinking and to guide your decision making in a manner that is optimal for them—and suboptimal for you.

I have worked with, and sometimes for, all of the entities that are risk elements in a project. I tell the real story about how these entities work, and how you can reduce the risk on your project by understanding the way in which they operate and the motivation and orientation of the information they provide. By knowing these entities so well, I can provide insight into how they think, the logic they will present to you, and what to do with this information.

Implementation Risk Management Versus Software Development Risk Management

Much of the academic literature on software risk management studies software development rather than software implementation. It's unclear why this is so, but overwhelmingly it is true. There were few quantitative studies on software risk management, with most papers being qualitative studies and anecdotes of how things are deemed to work to manage risk. One of the most influential writers in software risk management is Barry Boeher. Many of the research papers that I reviewed for this book referenced Barry Boeher. However, his background is software development rather than implementation. There are similarities between software development projects and software implementation projects, but there are important differences as well.

How Writing Bias Is Controlled at SCM Focus and SCM Focus Press

Bias is a serious problem in the enterprise software field. Large vendors receive uncritical coverage of their products, and large consulting companies recommend the large vendors that have the resources to hire and pay consultants rather than the vendors with the best software for the client's needs.

At SCM Focus, we have yet to financially benefit from a company's decision to buy an application showcased in print, either in a book or on the SCM Focus website. This may change in the future as SCM Focus grows—but we have been writing with a strong viewpoint for years without coming into any conflicts of interest. SCM Focus has the most stringent rules related to controlling bias and restricting commercial influence of any information provider. These "writing rules" are provided in the link below:

http://www.scmfocus.com/writing-rules/

If other information providers followed these rules, we would be able to learn about software without being required to perform our own research and testing for every topic.

Information about enterprise supply chain planning software can be found on the Internet, but this information is primarily promotional or written at such a high level that none of the important details or limitations of the application are exposed; this is true of books as well. When only one enterprise software application is covered in a book, one will find that the application works perfectly; the application operates as expected and there are no problems during the implementation to bring the application live. This is all quite amazing and quite different from my experience of implementing enterprise software. However, it is very difficult to make a living by providing objective information about enterprise supply chain software, especially as it means being critical at some point. I once remarked to a friend that SCM Focus had very little competition in providing untarnished information on this software category, and he said, "Of course, there is no money in it."

The Approach to the Book

By writing this book, I wanted to help people get exactly the information they need without having to read a lengthy volume. The approach to the book is essentially the same as to my previous books, and in writing this book I followed the same principles.

1. **Be direct and concise.** There is very little theory in this book and the math that I cover is simple. This book is focused on software and for most users and implementers of the software the most important thing to understand is conceptually what the software is doing.

2. **Based on project experience.** Nothing in the book is hypothetical; I have worked with it or tested it on an actual project. My project experience has led to my understanding a number of things that are not covered in typical supply planning books. In this book, I pass on this understanding to you.

The SCM Focus Site

As I am also the author of the SCM Focus site, http://www.scmfocus.com, the site and the book share a number of concepts and graphics. Furthermore, this book contains many links to articles on the site, which provide more detail on specific subjects.

Intended Audience
Primarily this book is directed at people who work for companies that implement enterprise software. This book is not for consultants or software vendors, as some of the information provided is designed to explain to clients how to receive better value from the various entities that provide information. Essentially, a person at an implementing company will be in a better position to do this after having read this book. If you have any questions or comments on the book, please e-mail me at shaunsnapp@scmfocus.com.

Abbreviations
A listing of all abbreviations used throughout the book is provided at the end of the book.

Corrections
Corrections and updates, as well as reader comments, can be viewed in the comment section of this book's web page. Also if you have comments or questions please add them to the page at the following link:

http://www.scmfocus.com/scmfocuspress/it-decision-making-books/enterprise-software-project-risk-management/

CHAPTER 2

Enterprise Software Risk Management Misconceptions

After a detailed analysis of this topic, it is clear that the standard approaches to managing risk on enterprise software selection and implementation projects such as hiring a name-brand consulting company, purchasing name-brand software, or paying for IT analysts like Gartner **do not work**.

While some journalists will bemoan the high failure rate of IT projects, they **fail** to point out the clear reasons why. Most of the advice they give and issues they highlight seem to just nibble around the edges of the problem. (Actually most journalists can't because the entities that are most responsible for the high failure rate of IT projects are major advertisers in the publications for which they write.).

Risk management starts at the top, and decisions made at the top are the most important to a project's outcome. However, executive decision-making is almost never the topic of risk management. Instead the focus tends to be on how to manage risks once poor decisions have already been made and after the options have narrowed considerably. That is not analytical risk management.

However, the failed approaches to risk management are still the dominant approaches for managing risk on software selection and implementation projects. This chapter explains why each approach does not work. We start off with one of the most common strategies.

Strategy 1: Purchasing Software from Large Software Vendors

Many purchasing companies think they will minimize risk by purchasing software from major "brand" software vendors. Both the large consulting companies and IT analysts are major proponents of this philosophy. I quote from the SCM Focus Press book *Gartner and the Magic Quadrant: A Guide for Buyers, Vendors and Investors,* which explains this bias toward large vendors quite clearly:

> *I am convinced that Gartner does not alter the numbers in its reports, but rather that Gartner selects a methodology that has the intended outcome of benefiting larger and more established vendors. Repeated observations of this outcome from a wide variety of Gartner reports make this conclusion unavoidable. However, it is unclear if this bias is due (either completely or partially) to the money paid by the largest vendors, or if Gartner is simply representing the interests of large buyers who tend to want to buy their software from larger vendors. Gartner knows its market very well, so it may simply be that Gartner has modeled their methodology based upon the criteria that large buyers themselves look for. To software-oriented people such as myself, the functionality of the application is the main focus, but to large corporations it is not the focus. Many other factors play into their decision.*
>
> *There are four main reasons that can be reasonably given for Gartner's large vendor bias.*
>
> 1. *Large vendors can pay more in consulting fees and for events than smaller vendors.*

2. *Larger vendors can allocate more people to working with Gartner and to knowing how to present the vendor's products to Gartner. The book* Up and to the Right—*which shows software vendors how to get high rankings—is at least some evidence that a high ranking is not based simply upon the quality of a vendor's software or "vision."*

3. *Most of the smaller software vendors are also much younger than the large software vendors and are simply not savvy to the analysts' game.*

4. *Gartner appears to base its research upon the preferences of the large buyers that are its core market, causing it to design its methodologies such that larger vendors perform better, independent of the actual software.*

Gartner and other IT analysts tell their clients repeatedly that buying software from larger software vendors **means less risk**. In fact, vendor size is a main factor in the criteria that make up their famous magic quadrant. But where is the evidence to support this viewpoint? This approach is based upon **perception** and the logical fallacy of *argumentum ad numerum* or *argumentum ad populum—that is, if many people believe something to be true, it must be true.* There are **no** studies that demonstrate that software from larger vendors is **less risky** than software from smaller vendors.[1] Let's think: what implementations have the highest failure rate in enterprise software? At Software Decisions, we researched ten enterprise software categories, and we estimated the some of the highest risk implementations to be from SAP and Oracle, who also happen to be the largest enterprise software vendors. This is the outcome of a number of factors. For instance, both SAP and Oracle primarily outsource their consulting work to the large consulting firms, who are less interested in taking projects live versus their primary objective of maximizing billing hours. SAS, another large software vendor has lower risk implementations for this reason—that is they implement most of their own software. Only rarely is the actual success rate of ERP implementations quoted, and when estimations are made, the quoted figures vary widely. According to the publication *The Critical Success Factors for ERP Implementation: An Organizational Fit Perspective*, the ERP success rate is roughly 25 percent. So, according to this source, 75 percent of ERP implementations are considered failures. But quoting

---

[1] This logical fallacy appeals to a widespread belief; the fact that many people believe it means it must be true.

just one study is misleading because the estimates are truly all over the map, as the following quote attests.

> *"A study by the Standish Group estimates that 31 percent of projects are not successful (Kamhawi, 2007). Barker and Frolick (2003) suggest that 50 percent of ERP implementations are failures. Hong and Kim (2002) estimate a 75 percent failure rate, while Scott and Vessey (2002) estimate failure rates as high as 90 percent. Different statistics for the success or failure of ERP projects have been offered by researchers. In addition Bradford and Sandy (2002) reported that 57 percent of the companies they interviewed had not attempted to assess the performance of their ERP systems owing to a lack of empirically effective evaluation models."*
>
> — Measures of Success in Project Implementing Enterprise
> Resource Planning

Various research studies produce different values, but the range is between a failure rate of 75 percent and 50 percent, and a 90 percent chance of going **178 percent over the implementation budget**. There are other reasons for the high risk of SAP and Oracle, including quality control issues at SAP as well as the problems that come with so many acquisitions on the part of Oracle. However, this topic has a number of dimensions and could go on for some time, so the fact remains that Gartner cannot produce any evidence that larger vendors mean less risk. Both SAP and Oracle are the largest ERP vendors in the world and their ERP implementations go south all the time. I personally evaluate SAP ERP implementations years after they have been implemented and find the supply chain areas of the system quite sub-optimized, and these are on "successful" implementations. Therefore, this emphasis on software vendor size by Gartner is nothing more than a bias. Let's remember that the largest software vendors pay Gartner more than the smaller vendors. So vendor size reflects positively in Gartner's revenues, and this, of course, causes them to reflect positively in Gartner's reviews.

As a person who has worked in the enterprise software industry since 1997, and has worked with software vendors of all sizes, I can say that large vendors actually have a number of **disadvantages** that increase their risk. First, larger software vendors tend to provide lower quality information than smaller software vendors to their customers. Software Decisions assigns the "Quality of Information Provided" score to every software vendor that is evaluated. Performing a regression between the Quality of Information Provided and the size of the software vendor shows a negative relationship between the size of the software vendor and quality of information provided. A major reason for this is the constant need for growth. I once worked for i2 Technologies (a supply chain planning software vendor), and as this company grew, its marketing information and what it told customers diverged from reality. i2 Technologies had another disease—the disease of acquisition—which is often caused by meeting the needs of the stock market to show growth larger than could be accomplished with sales of internally developed applications. i2 Technologies purchased software vendors that appeared to me to be stock scams. One of the most ridiculous was the purchase of a company called Aspect for roughly $9.3 billion in overpriced i2 Technologies stock. Here is the quotation from Sanjiv Sidhu, the CEO of i2 Technologies at the time of the acquisition back in March 2000.

> *"'The merger will create a B2B marketplace powerhouse with unmatched solution breadth and depth of functionality, unparalleled content, and a laser-focus on value creation,' added Sanjiv Sidhu."*

The merger accomplished none of these things. The result of the acquisition: a major goose egg. Aspect never contributed to i2 Technologies in a meaningful way, but I was forced to sit through various indoctrination sessions of why there were such tremendous "synergies," and why content management was so critical to supply chain planning (it isn't).

Acquisitions are major distractions for almost any company; however they are particularly problematic for a software vendor. The quality of applications produced by a software vendor is primarily determined by the cohesion of the company and its ability to bring the right knowledge to bear in the right area at the right time and in the right quantity. Acquisitions lead individuals to overseeing, selling and working on applications that **they don't understand**. Acquisitions are never pretty, as the management of the acquiring company tends to condescend to and dis-empower the leadership of company being acquired, causing many of them to leave. Furthermore, in the software vendors that are tracked by Software Decisions, there is a correlation between software vendors that grow through acquisitions and the reduced sustainability of these companies.

I have also noticed that major enterprise software vendors like SAP and Oracle are much more focused on marketing and developing "partnerships" than on improving the quality of their software. Basically, they are looking to build a social network rather than compete on your software. Marketing is a necessary function, but it can't be the **primary focus** of a software company, and the marketing and sales can't get ahead of an application's capabilities. This is exactly what happened at i2 Technologies when I worked there. I recall protesting against the tactics that i2 Technologies was using to a person in a senior position in the company, and them answering my argument with, *"You have to understand, this is how things are done. This is how SAP and Oracle do things, and is why they are so successful."*

Secondly, large software vendors lag behind the smaller software vendors in terms of innovation. I have worked with SAP products since 1997. My exposure ranges from SAP ERP to the advanced planning suite—for which I have written five books—business intelligence, SAP MDM, SAP XI and many other SAP applications. Never once in all my work with SAP have I found **anything innovative** in the software. The advanced planning suite is actually a copy of what I was doing at i2 Technologies back in the late 1990s. This should not be surprising as SAP developed a "partnership" with i2 Technologies, then broke off the partnership and walked out with a lot of intellectual property so they could build their SAP APO advanced planning suite. Similarly Oracle is not known for innovation, and within a couple of years of acquiring a company (and Oracle has acquired quite a few) the acquired application is no longer seen as a leading application. As with other monopolies, monopolistic software vendors do not need to innovate and do not need to improve their products because they pay large consulting companies and IT analysts to pitch their software for them. This lack of innovation is explained in detail in the following article.

http://www.scmfocus.com/enterprisesoftwarepolicy/2012/03/11/why-the-largest-enterprise-software-companies-have-no-reason-to-innovate/

Larger software vendors translate almost directly to more bureaucracy and slower response times. I work with software from both the largest and the smallest software vendors, and after many years this generalization is entirely obvious[2] and furthermore, it applies to every software category because it is the nature of bureaucracy. Smaller software vendors are a pleasure to deal with because you can get fast and honest answers to questions about how things work in the application and what is coming down the pike. Larger software vendors, on the other hand, are often miserable to deal with. The larger a software vendor, the more layers and the more bureaucracy. This bureaucracy has a serious cost, which ends up being **imposed** upon the buyers. The bureaucracy means the buyer must be more persistent in following up on information requests. Responses to the requests will take longer, and on average the responses are less reliable because larger companies are more political. For instance, the support staff of large software vendors—which may in fact be outsourced—goes through political training so as to not provide honest answers that might make the sales department look bad. It also means that the buyer must pay more money for consultants to spend more time trying to find the answers to questions. I have been one of those consultants, and I have a PhD in getting the runaround from several large vendors on technical queries. When I work with a smaller software vendor, I often know the person in support personally, and get a definitive answer usually with a single e-mail. When I deal with a software behemoth like SAP, I contact a support person I have never met, who most often lives in a low-cost country that has English as a second language, and have to go back and forth with that person as he or she describes how to test things I have already tested. This second process can take weeks.

Software Decisions has profiled many applications, and this research is conclusive: purchasing from a large software vendor is not a valid strategy for reducing risk. In fact, the relationship is a negative one: on average, applications purchased from

---

[2] An amazing story of inefficiency and its relationship to software vendor size is Microsoft. Microsoft has 90,000 employees; what is the actual average output of each employee? Microsoft owns a group of applications that it developed years ago. Almost all of Microsoft's products were copied from other competitor applications (the Office Suite, Bing, SQL Server, SharePoint, etc.); therefore the creative output at Microsoft has always been quite low. Of these applications, none of them improve much from year to year, and sometimes they step backward (as was the case with Windows 8, an operating system where Microsoft had years to simply copy the Apple IOS or Android OS and yet still could not get it right). This means 90,000 employees—most of whom are well educated and motivated and capable of creative work—do very little of it because of the entity they work for.

larger software vendors are riskier to implement than applications purchased from smaller software vendors. Software development is not an area that is subject to economies of scale, such as with a power plant or a telephone network. In fact, diseconomies of scale are far more prevalent. The most innovative and highest quality software tends to come from the smallest, not the largest, software vendors.

Strategy 2: Purchasing More Software from One Software Vendor

The second strategy is an augmentation of the first. However, its logic is based primarily upon integration, which historically has been the "fools gold" in the enterprise software area.

The concept is that the buyer will receive benefits through improved integration if they buy **more** software from a single vendor. This is how companies end up with applications that are inappropriate and have low functionality, and, in fact, it is one of the primary methods by which large software vendors and mediocre applications compete with, and win out against, far superior applications. The perception of integration benefits were instrumental in the growth of ERP systems. I quote from my book *The Real Story Behind ERP: Separating Fiction from Reality*:

> *Enhanced integration was one of the major selling points of ERP. The hours of PowerPoint presentations that have been created since the first ERP systems were sold describe the great cost savings and integrative benefits that implementing companies would receive from a "solution" where all the main applications used the same database. One of the assumptions about purchasing an ERP system was that the buying company would implement all of the modules and decommission their current software.*

> *The fact is, some of the company's pre-existing applications could not be replaced by ERP, and for a variety of very good reasons.*

> *Contrary to most assumptions, ERP systems provide no advantages in terms of integration to other systems, and in fact present several disadvantages.*

Here is a much more effective solution than I have described above: ERP vendors should never have been allowed to procure other vendors. They should not have created external applications, and instead should have published an integration standard and allowed the middleware vendors (those that were actually skilled at creating middleware) to create the adapters.

> *"ERP technology does not offer an integrated solution but amplifies the need for integration."*
>
> — ERP and Application Integration

> *"Although ERP is touted as a single architecture, ERP applications usually contain different generations and sources of technology. Third-party applications are acquired and amalgamated into the platform, sometimes by name only. In total, this makes the environment complex for the customer and difficult to change over time. ERP suppliers have become **system integrators.** [emphasis added] The sheer size and number of applications makes moving all the applications forward a difficult task. Application functionality often lags."*
>
> — ERP Alternatives

As it turns out, the hypothesis (and it was never anything other than a untested hypothesis, no matter how confidently it has been asserted) that selecting more software from one vendor reduces the integration costs has not worked at all in practice. There is no research to support their assertion. (Hint: At Software Decisions we did perform the research, and the assertion turns out to be incorrect.) Furthermore, the approach of purchasing software from the same vendor places unnecessary shackles on the software selection process. SAP and Oracle have grown to their dominant position by exploiting this hypothesis, and it has caused many software vendors such as JDA, Sage and Infor to acquire software in the hopes of providing a full suite of products to customers, steering their customers to purchase other applications, often on the basis of the software vendor that provides the ERP system. These vendors see the ERP system as the pathway to achieving more monopoly power to increasing their prices.[3]

Buyers who follow this strategy often find that the integration promised during the sales process is **far less** than advertised. This is true of SAP for which it has a longstanding policy to overstate the degree of integration between its applications. The following article is a description of the many integration problems between SAP ERP ECC/R/3 and SAP APO; however, the same problem generalizes to other SAP products.

> http://www.scmfocus.com/sapplanning/2011/05/19/why-i-no-longer-recommend-using-the-cif/

Certainly this policy is not limited to SAP. Instead it is one of the major sales misrepresentations/strategies of large software vendors. For software vendors such as Oracle, JDA and Infor that have grown through acquisition, their "suites" provide very little integration benefit over purchasing a variety of applications from unrelated software vendors. Each application attained by these serial acquirers has its own heritage, unrelated to the heritage of the acquiring vendor. Therefore the integration "benefits" that are promised so aggressively during the sales process are mostly an illusion. All that happens is that the buyer creates a faster implementation time projection, the duration of which must be changed during the implementation itself. However, while the integration benefits are illusory, the buyer absolutely loses out on the more applicable functionality that could be obtained by making a truly competitive process out of the software selection.

Our research at Software Decisions shows that buying a large quantity of software from one vendor is actually the worst strategy that a company can follow, as it results in the highest costs and lowest functionality of all available solution architecture strategies. We also measure the riskiness of applications, and again,

---

[3] The term "monopoly power" does not mean that there is only one seller in the marketplace. This tends to confuse many people, but when economists use the term "monopoly power," they do not mean that a company is a perfect monopoly. Every firm can be evaluated upon a continuum, where at one end is perfect competition, and the other is perfect monopoly. Increasing one's monopoly power (which is frequently accomplished in the software industry through acquisitions and partnerships with large consulting companies) simply moves the company further to the right on this continuum toward perfect monopoly.

the more applications that are purchased from one vendor, the higher the risk to the buyer, as the likelihood of implementing a weak application increases. The strength of a large software vendor's many applications is not consistent across all of their applications. The more a buyer purchases from any one vendor, the higher the likelihood that the buyer will purchase an application that has a far more competitive alternative out in the marketplace—one that can be implemented more quickly, at lower risk, and with a higher ROI.

This research is shown in an article at the following link:

> http://www.scmfocus.com/softwaredecisions/plans/solution-architecture-packages/

Strategy 3: Relying Upon Large IT Consulting Companies

Another commonly used strategy is to hire a major consulting company to provide selection advice. Universally, large consulting companies propose that clients should listen to them and trust their advice. They say that they have the right answers to enterprise software questions and further, that they serve their clients' interests. Although not explicitly stated, there is the implied assumption that each major consulting company will recommend applications and vendors that are both **appropriate for the business requirements** but are of a **reasonable risk level**.

Is this actually true? Is there a way to test this hypothesis? The question we had was whether clients that followed the advice of major consulting companies would receive the benefit of lower risk implementations. As it turns out, there is a way to test this. The applications recommended by the major consulting companies are rated for risk (among other characteristics such as maintainability, usability, functionality and implement-ability) in the Software Decisions *MUFI Rating & Risk* evaluation. We compared the *MUFI Rating & Risk* evaluation for applications in ten software categories and compared them to software that the major consulting companies typically recommend.

Those who do not work in the field might think that the advice cannot be tracked as it would vary per client. However, the advice offered by the major consulting companies does not vary. They have large IT consulting practices that are built primarily around recommending and implementing the same applications: those offered by SAP and Oracle. Both SAP and Oracle offer most of their consulting business to the major consulting companies, who in turn recommend their software. The major consulting companies then turn around and tell their clients that they are offering them "objective and considered advice."

The Research Results

The research shows that the applications recommended by the major consulting companies always have **a high or the highest TCO (total cost of ownership)** in the respective software category, along with the **highest risk**. The reason is simple: not a single major consulting company that provides IT services is a fiduciary. This means Accenture, IBM, Deloitte, etc., have no legal responsibility to place their client's interests ahead of their own. And the internal incentives laid out within each consulting company, where sales is far more esteemed than implementing the software successfully, or even implementing the best software (there is no measure for this whatsoever) means that the customer's interests are a distant second to the profit maximizing interest of the consulting company. It is in the financial self-interest of these major consulting companies to recommend software for which they have trained resources **ready to bill**—therefore it is this software that is recommended. What might be right for their clients simply does not enter into the equation. What is the formula you might ask?

Large Company Advice = Course of Action Followed by the Client which Maximizes Billing Revenue

Clients may think they are getting objective advice, when in fact, the advice has been predetermined based upon the consulting company's financial incentives. The agreement made between the major consulting companies and SAP and Oracle is carried out without the client's knowledge. It's a *quid pro quo* and the conversation between the two goes a something like this:

"You give us the recommendation—we give you the consulting business."

It should not be difficult to make the logical leap that if enterprise software buyers rely upon advisors that are corrupt and do not have their clients' interests at heart, everyone's risk for software implementations will be increased.

Large consulting companies not only provide untrustworthy information to their clients, they greatly **increase the costs** of the implementation. First, they charge very high rates for their consultants. Secondly, this advice results in the buyer making poor-quality decisions that increase overall IT costs and lessen their ability to satisfy business requirements. One might ask why this rather obvious relationship between Oracle and SAP and the major consulting companies is never discussed in well-known IT periodicals such as *CIO*. I will give you one guess as to the names of the two largest advertisers in *CIO*.

Strategy 4: Using a Single Prime Contractor

The use of a prime contractor is a frequently employed strategy that is commonly thought to mitigate risk, but like many risk mitigation strategies, no evidence is ever presented that it **actually does** mitigate risk. The logic behind this myth is that risk is reduced if there are fewer points of risk—fewer parties that are ultimately responsible for the risk on the contractor side. This logic comes from a basic misunderstanding about the behavior of most prime contractors.

Many buyers prefer to hire a single prime contractor to implement their projects (and not just IT projects). This prime contractor is typically a large consulting company. The buyer feels better thinking that they will have a single party to hold accountable, or as the terrible saying goes, "one throat to choke."

This strategy has driven buyers to reduce the number of entities that they hire directly, meaning the approved vendor list is very short, and quite often shockingly immune to the actual performance of the suppliers or large consulting firms. I am aware of one client who uses only CSC or Accenture for its IT work, both of which have provided very poor value to this buyer for a number of years. As much as the project managers at this buyer may complain about the performance of these firms, they have **no latitude** to choose another firm. To this buyer, "competition" means switching the IT contracts between the different firms.

This exact issue—a very limited number of suppliers being called upon by an enterprise software buyer—arose during the now well-known HealthCare.gov website fiasco. The company that won the HealthCare.gov contract initially, CGI, had underperformed on US government contracts for many years, but this did not stop them from receiving the HealthCare.gov contract. When the problems regarding the website became well-known, some people connected the dots when they figured out who had received the contract. CGI is a big firm, but even though the initial failure of HeathCare.gov is in little doubt, the government will not receive **money back from CGI;** instead the government paid CGI in full.

This is one of the great myths of hiring a prime contractor—that the prime contractor in some way "guarantees the project." While certainly this impression is given during the sales process, oral statements about supporting the project or being dedicated to the project don't mean much. What actually matters is how the consulting contracts are worded; the contracts created by prime contractors protect them from liability quite well. How do they do this you might ask? Typically the prime contractors are responsible for meeting milestones—which they often control as they frequently manage the project—but almost never are they on the hook for the **performance** of the system.

During the HealthCare.gov scandal, Obama complained that the government should analyze the way IT contracts are bid. Apparently he meant that the way IT contracts are bid for will be analyzed by **some other** administration, because when Accenture received the contract to fix the site and CGI's contract was not renewed, it **was not** a competitive bid. In fact, the bid process was managed in the same way that the awarding of the initial contract to CGI was managed, which was also not a competitive bid. The reason given is the same as was given for many of the corrupt bids that were handed out to defense contractors during the second Gulf War—that there was simply **no time** because aggressive timelines would have to be met. Interestingly, Accenture has one of the poorer reputations for implementation success, and a **poorer** reputation as an implementer than CGI. However, the government and most private companies cannot even think about giving contracts to anyone other than "the usual suspects," because both CGI and Accenture lobby the government heavily for contracts, with CGI alone receiving $8 billion in government contracts. These are firms that control the flow of contracts in their direction by paying off government decision-makers in one way or another. According to OpenSecrets, since 2006 CGI has paid $800,000 on a variety of contracts—a very small amount of money when compared to many other firms, particularly defense contractors. However, even these values underestimate the effect of lobbying, as highly placed employees rotate between the government and these private entities, meaning that if you are a government decision-maker, awarding contracts to the right private entity can often mean a very well-paying job and job security when you have completed your "rotation" through "public service."

All of these reasons are why the prior performance of these companies—which one may think naively would be paramount to the decision-making process—does not seem to control decision making. CGI had experienced multiple problems in creating health care registries before it received the HealthCare.gov contract. CGI has had successful implementations but there is little doubt that CGI was **nowhere close** to the best company to award the contract for HealthCare.gov. The best company or series of companies would have been smaller web development companies without making any one of them the prime contractor. However, because these types of companies do not have sufficient lobbying muscle, they can't win these types of contracts, something that is explained by the following quotation:

"Evan Burfield, who founded the relatively small company that worked with CGI to build Recovery.gov, says the problem lies more in a federal procurement apparatus that makes it nearly impossible for an agile newcomer to bid on projects that in the private sector would take much less time and money. Plus, with so many contractors, everyone could technically fulfill the requirements in their statement of work, and the thing can still not work in the end."[4]

The uncompetitive nature of the contracting process for IT services is **not** unique to the government. These same consulting firms that sell to the public sector also sell to the private sector. This point was missed by pro-private sector or pro "free market" voices, who assigned blame for the botched HealthCare.gov website on the fact that it was a government project. However, these voices emanated from

---

[4] Depillis, Lydia, Meet CGI Federal, the Company Behind the Botched Launch of HealthCare.gov. *The Washington Post*. October 16, 2013.

entities that either did not understand how the system worked, or who knew but were deliberately providing misleading information in their statements. CGI is a private company, not a government entity. Secondly, botched IT implementations are incredibly common in the private sector, just as they are in the public sector. Certainly, the project's overseeing agency, the Department of Health and Human Services, put the project in a difficult situation by not completing the requirements in a way that gave CGI enough time to complete the website's creation; however, many private sector companies that I have worked for have been guilty of doing the same thing. In fact, I cannot recall a project where the complaint was not made at some point that either the requirements took too long to gather, or when they were gathered, they were either incomplete or not sufficiently documented.

The unfortunate fact is that, when it comes to acquiring IT contracts, who one knows is far more important than the firm's performance. Both the government and the private sector could receive much better value by changing their IT procurement approach, and they could do so very easily. One of the easiest ways is to simply stop awarding contracts to large consulting companies as prime contractors. They could replace these firms by building their own teams of contractors or hiring smaller consulting firms, but they **choose to drive** most of the business to the giant consulting firms. Smaller firms and independent contractors are more motivated to provide good work because they do not have the brand names and lobbying or sales muscle to repeatedly obtain contracts after not performing well on previous contracts.

The Reality of Setting Up Prime Contractors

While it might be a nice idea to hire a prime contractor (often a massive consulting conglomerate) and let the prime contractor hire subcontractors, it does not work for software implementations.[5] This strategy is deployed frequently, but as with any strategy being relied upon to reduce risk, it's important to ask whether evidence exists to prove it's a good strategy. Here are the well-documented reasons as to why the prime contractor model is flawed:

1. *Control Over Advice Offered by Subcontractors:* The prime contractor model results in the subcontractors serving the desires of the prime contractor

---

[5] Some of the best software values are from smaller software vendors that do not have the project management staffing or size to really take on a prime contractor role.

(often having their opinions censored by the prime contractor, which has happened to me on several occasions as a subcontractor) instead of serving the desires of the end client. This fact should be entirely obvious at this point, and those buyers that have not realized this are simply not paying attention.

2. *Lack of Disclosure:* The large consulting companies have many partnerships and arrangements that work against their clients' interests and of which their clients have no knowledge. When one has a financial relationship with another entity that could work against the interests of one's client, that relationship is supposed to be disclosed. However, the major consulting companies never disclose these relationships. Larger consulting companies have more of these financial relationships than smaller consulting companies, making the accuracy of their advice quite dubious.

3. *Legal Contracts Overprotect the Prime Contractor:* The end client receives precious little risk mitigation benefit because the legal contracts written by the prime contractor essentially **remove themselves from legal liability.** Major consulting companies are so habituated to dissatisfied clients that they have managing them down to a science, including the legal aspect.

While the prime contractor model is durable and widely deployed, there is no evidence that using a prime contractor reduces risk, and, in fact, there is considerable evidence that it does not. Buyers should replace simplistic platitudes such as "one throat to choke,"[6] with an actual analysis of the history of the prime contractor model. If they do this research, they will find that this model actually increases risk. Managing IT projects is not something that can be outsourced. A successful model is one where the buyer takes an active management role in the project, but hires the necessary expertise that they do not have in-house.

Strategy 5: Relying Upon IT Analysts

One of the issues that smaller vendors encounter regularly is the built-in assumptions about smaller vendors that no one has ever proven to be true. One can rely upon quite a few IT analysts for advice, but Gartner is by far the most influential and important IT analyst in the enterprise software space.

---

[6] This platitude assumes that one throat to choke is actually a choke-able throat.

Possibly the most significant thing to understand about Gartner is that they are the pre-eminent marketing company in their space. At their heart they are an information broker, as the following quotation explains.

> *Gartner's issuance of a report really means something significant to corporate buyers, and has real financial consequences for those vendors mentioned in the report, both good and bad. Gartner is in the catbird seat desired by many companies in that they are able to charge for information that many of the vendors pay to give them. Gartner is paid while it both gathers information and provides advice. Gartner is so influential that they control (in part) the fates of software vendors and set specific standards to which software vendors must adhere. Gartner has a series of preferences to which vendors either adhere or pay a penalty in the marketplace.*
> —Gartner and the Magic Quadrant

In short, Gartner is almost always getting paid. Those interested in a full accounting of Gartner can see my book *Gartner and the Magic Quadrant: A Guide for Buyers, Vendors and Investors.*

Gartner is highly influential in **selling** their analytical output, but their influence does not end there. Gartner is very effective at influencing **thought** patterns of a high percentage of those involved in enterprise software decisions. Unbeknownst to these decision makers, Gartner has a strong large vendor bias. What may be interesting to many is that Gartner never performs research into what represents **high or low risk** with respect to the many enterprise applications that they analyze. In its analysis, it simply uses a vendor's size as a proxy for the risk level of any application. However, as I hope the previous sections have illustrated, vendor size is in fact inversely related to risk.

My research into this area has led me to conclude that Gartner does not analyze risk in any realistic way for the following reasons.

1. *Its Political Implications:* Gartner does not have any interest in performing the research because it would be a political hot potato with software

vendors. Gartner actively sells consulting services to the same software vendors that it rates.

2. *Specifics of Their Vendor Revenue Stream:* Gartner is paid money by big vendors—and if Gartner did the research they would find the results are the **opposite** of their financial interests. It is not coincidence that Gartner tends to promote the idea that larger software vendors reduce implementation risk.

And it's not just Gartner, but other IT analysts as well that do not quantify risk. Not only is risk not quantified, but most of the other factors important to those making implementation decisions are not quantified either, such as costs, durations, manpower, etc. By using an IT analyst, a buyer is more likely to apply the same risk criteria used by that IT analyst. However, there is no evidence that these risk criteria—which primarily have to do with the largeness of the software vendor or the implementation consulting company—actually work.

Introduction to Support Staffing Level Planning

There is precious little information on the appropriate support staffing level for enterprise software, other than data from surveys. These surveys simply report on what the leaders in IT organizations say their staffing levels are, and what their staffing levels actually are. Generally these staffing surveys do not differentiate between various types of applications in terms of their staffing requirements. For instance, some applications like CRM are far less complex than business intelligence applications, for example, and inherently require less support. This is why, at Software Decisions, a support level is customized per application as is based upon the **input provided** to the interactive online TCO Calculator.

Normally buyers do not estimate the staffing level of new applications, and have a strong tendency to treat all applications within the same category as requiring the **same** support staffing. This is a mistake; our research at Software Decisions takes into account the fact that the level of support required varies considerably across applications, even within a single software category. For instance, because companies do not normally estimate differential support staffing, often they will end up selecting applications that have a high support load. A good example of this is when a buyer chooses to purchase an application that is not a strong match for their business requirements; the application is purchased for some other reason, such as it is "integrated" to other applications that they already own from the same vendor. In cases where the fit to the business requirements is low, buyers must customize this application more, which leads to higher support staffing requirements.

Applications with lower usability also lead to more support requests—and therefore higher staffing requirements. Therefore, one of the best ways to end up with high-maintenance applications is to not estimate the support load of the applications being evaluated for purchase and instead to think it will all even out in the end. For a number of years we have evaluated enterprise software implementations post go-live, and every application could benefit from more support and many applications are in a state of disrepair. It's one thing to develop a large amount of functionality; it is quite another to implement the functionality and keep it working at a good level for a number of years.

Among many reasons, the under-supported nature of enterprise software is related to factors such as the:

- *Complexity:* The inherent complexity of enterprise software

- *Funding:* The funding available for its support

- *The Information from the Sales Process:* Overselling of functionality by both software vendors and consulting companies

- *Functionality to Business Requirements Mismatch:* Implementation of functionality that was not really the right functionality for the business requirements

In fact, the continual underperformance of enterprise software versus its potential is a very strong argument for deploying SaaS applications more widely. SaaS has considerable maintenance benefits in addition to implementation benefits. For every application category that we track at Software Decisions, maintenance and support is by far the highest TCO cost. Usually this cost is underestimated because increasingly support costs are incurred by the business and not by IT support. A primary reason for this is the move to outsourcing, which is the topic of the next section.

Strategy 6: Low Support Staffing and Outsourcing

I want to be clear that buyers who implement enterprise software **do not** employ low support staffing **nor** do they outsource their IT support as part of a "strategy" to reduce risk. However, these are two strategies that have a very important impact on the risk of any enterprise software application, and therefore I thought it important to cover these topics. There is an impression that these two strategies are unrelated to software risk. At Software Decisions we categorize risk into three areas: the application risk, the vendor risk, and the client-specific risk—which contains several subcategories of risk. Support staffing falls into this third risk category.

As I discussed in the introduction of Strategy 6: Support Staffing Level Planning, there is little research into IT support staffing. In the rather limited surveys, respondents—who usually are highly placed individuals in IT organizations—state that IT support staffing is roughly half of the optimal staffing.

Interestingly, the staffing level considered optimal seems too low according to the staffing levels that we develop at Software Decisions, averaged across all of the software categories that we cover. Our staffing levels are different because in our view, it is not at all surprising that executives underestimate the staffing required because those who work in IT fill out these surveys. IT often thinks in terms of responding to support **tickets**. If the issue is opened and the ticket can be closed, to IT this is a successful transaction. And it is, but only within a limited context. Simply responding to support requests by fixing immediate issues does not allow a company to fully leverage the application. Our ratios are not based upon the minimum staff required to keep support tickets at a moderate level, but upon the staffing level that we think is necessary to allow the company to leverage the application and meet a significant ROI on their overall investment. ROI is often why the application was justified for purchase in the first place, although often no financial model provides the financial justification.

Shortcomings in support staffing are a major factor as to why buyers gain a far smaller portion of an application's value. Buyers are assisted in their underestimation of support requirements by software vendors who almost universally give them the wrong impression that their software is far easier to use and maintain than it generally is. I quote from the Software Decisions *Software Category Analysis for Business Intelligence*:

> *One of the biggest trends in BI has been the move to so-called "self-service." The efficiency of IT with regards to report creation has been well understood to be* **poor**, *with literally applications like SAP BI and IBM Cognos pulling the life force out of the business with late reports, or reports that are provided that do not meet the business requirements. The support ratios for many applications in business intelligence are so high that they are driving buyers to applications with lower support ratios. IT is in a conundrum with respect to BI. They have a natural inclination to want to control BI, to choose the solution, but on the other hand, they are tired of being beat up for reports being late—a perpetual issue at most buyers that we interact with. However the term self-service is a heavily marketing laden term. None of the applications that are often called self-service are actually self-service to the extent that they actually do not require significant training and hand holding. Applications, which are described as self-service by the business, press and by software vendors and IT analysts like Gartner—are simply lower support requirement applications.*

A good example of this is Tableau. Tableau is an innovation leader in the business intelligence space. They provide an application that is very powerful and can allow properly trained and experienced resources to create all manner of reports using interesting relationships. We have reviewed some of Tableau's reports, and these have taught us very important relationships. Tableau's front end has an excellent design and is a thing of beauty.

However, while it is marketed as such, Tableau is **not** a self-service application. It requires significant training as well as support in order for it to work its magic.

Tableau is **more** self-service than many other BI applications, but that is not saying a lot as many BI applications are horrendously complicated and design disasters. However, many executive decision-makers think they can take Tableau, provide their users with limited training, and have them creating deeply illustrative reports all based upon the inherent capabilities of Tableau.

At Software Decisions, our review of the business intelligence software category shows that this focus on self-service is going to lead to greatly understaffed business intelligence support, which will lead to many problems after this new batch of "self-service" applications go live. Unfortunately, these facts do not come across in the sales phase, leading buyers of Tableau to underestimate the support-staffing requirement.

Outsourced Support

Outsourcing IT support is one of the great trends in IT support and has been for some time. Certainly there are cost advantages to outsourcing IT support; however, the problem with the information on IT outsourcing is that it comes from entities that benefit financially from outsourcing.

All of the major consulting companies write papers on outsourcing. They provide a very one-sided perspective on the value of outsourcing to potential customers. None of the papers I reviewed mentioned the fact that the entity itself had a large outsourcing business, and that this may bias the conclusions that they reached in their papers. Every company that I have consulted with and that has outsourced their IT department has run into major communication and cultural issues. Secondly, an outsourced department does not have the same history or experience with the business as an internal IT department. Thus, it takes them much longer to understand the tickets submitted by the business and to interpret them. Because of a lack of familiarity with many of the company's systems and specific configurations or customizations, they are at a serious disadvantage in troubleshooting, estimation, understanding how various systems interact, and so on.

Another issue with outsourcing is the middleman. The major consulting firms are getting wealthy from outsourcing because they take a big cut of the contract.

Interestingly, many of these large consulting companies can't seem to manage their outsourcing resources. In many cases, the Indian firm or placement agency is taking a big cut as well, meaning that not nearly as much is left over as the company thinks is left over to pay for the work being done. I do not have the invoices to show who is getting paid what, but I strongly suspect that this is a primary reason as to why most outsourcing operations provide such a low level of service and why these operations experience such high turnover, as the more experienced support personnel move out of support roles at the first opportunity.

The level of support I have witnessed from outsourced IT organizations is incredibly poor. The management seems consistently haphazard, bringing to mind the management efficiency of the US government's disaster response to Hurricane Katrina.

In many cases the business feels as if they have no support, and they begin hiring their own IT people to develop short cuts for them. Essentially, outsourced IT breaks the labor specialization within the company as the business has to in part become its own IT support. This is one reason that the use of spreadsheets and offline Access databases is not decreasing after all the years of implementing enterprise systems. The business is finding that they have to develop offline tools because the basic maintenance of enterprise systems is not performed correctly.

Simply stated, outsourced IT increases the risk incurred by companies on every implementation and with every application for which support is outsourced. It is certainly desirable to save money, but quality is of course a consideration. The main reason as to why support continues to be outsourced is that the management of IT is more incentivized to reduce costs than they are to support the business effectively.

Conclusion

This chapter identified and covered six different commonly employed but ineffective strategies in managing enterprise software risk. These strategies are myths, and have never been proven to be true. However they are supported by entities that personally financially benefit from buyers believing in them. As the famous quotation from Josh Billings goes, *"It ain't ignorance causes so much trouble; it's folks knowing so much that ain't so.*" In order for buyers to truly manage their project risk, they must critically analyze these strategies. I have done so in this chapter, so readers must decide if I have provided enough evidence to at least make them pause before blindly relying upon these strategies. In all of my years in IT, I do not recall anyone providing any evidence that the assumptions underlying these strategies are true, rather they are simply repeated.

CHAPTER 3

The Basics of Enterprise Software Risk Management

To understand how to manage IT project risks, we must first define what we mean by risk. There are many different degrees of success or failure on a project. Any attempt to pick a specific value of success results in an interpretive approach that simply places an implementation on a continuum between the best and worst possible outcomes. While this system is universally loved by users, it drives continuous business improvement to the abject failure side of the continuum where the software must be implemented from scratch, and a consulting company is either fired, or fired and sued.

The failure or success rate of enterprise software projects is frequently quoted. Articles on enterprise software risk or success often state that around 50 percent of enterprise software projects are considered successful, and therefore 50 percent are considered failures. Another frequently quoted statistic is that around 35 percent of projects are generally considered to be able to show **quantifiable** business benefit.

While these types of statistics are frequently quoted, how these statistics were arrived at in the first place is almost never discussed. As background research for this book, I reviewed all of the literature on process success and failure. It turns out that the quoted statistics make the research sound far more conclusive than it actually is. In effect journalists are quoting the work of previous journalists, but they are not going back and reading the original research. Therefore many of the authors on this topic lack an authentic understanding of the research they are quoting. This would not be a problem if the original research was unambiguous, but it is in fact quite ambiguous. The following quotation illustrates the ambiguity of much of this research.

> *"According to the estimation of the Standish Group International,*
> *90 percent of SAP R/3 ERP projects run late, another SGI study*
> *of 7400 IT projects revealed that 34 percent were late or over budget,*
> *31 percent were abandoned, scaled back or modified, and only*
> *24 percent were completed on time and on budget. One explanation*
> *for the high ERP project failure rate is that managers do not take*
> *prudent measures to assess and manage the risks involved in these*
> *projects."*
>
> —Risk Assessment in ERP Projects

These statistics are guidelines, but I don't consider them anywhere near as useful as many journalists seem to think they are. Of course how journalists interpret the statistics depends on if you think they actually reviewed anything beyond the statistic they read in the magazine. Some important questions to ask with respect to studies on project success are the following:

1. *What is the Definition of Success?:* Different studies have different definitions of a successful implementation, and many of these types of classification statistics depend upon how survey questions are asked. The surveys also assume that the respondents **know** themselves if the project was in fact successful (which I addressed earlier). Also, what exactly is "successful"? For instance, if a project showing a 15 percent ROI easily could have shown a 20 percent ROI if certain simple changes were made, was the project successful? If the software that was replaced was truly providing poor output, then is this the same as if the new software was selected simply because

a new CIO was hired and was simply more comfortable with a different vendor? Success is contextual, based upon the next change between the output quality prior to the implementation go live—and the output quality post implementation go live.

2. *The Percentage of Functionality Used:* Another frequently used, but ultimately unhelpful marker of implementation success is the percentage of the software's functionality used by the company. For example, if a company uses 10 percent of the functionality offered by an application, that sounds bad, doesn't it? However, if that is all the functionality required by the company, and if the ROI is still positive, then this would not seem to be a problem. There is simply no way to determine success on the basis of some percentage of functionality used, and even assigning a percentage of functionality used is tricky.

3. *Meeting Deadlines:* The sad conclusion of research into how enterprise software implementation success is rated, is that most companies base success primarily upon whether an implementation **met** project deadlines. This is explained by the following quotation.

> *"According to Parr and Shanks (2000), 'ERP project success simply means bringing the project in on time and on budget.' So, most ERP projects start with a basic management drive to target faster implementation and a more cost-effective project.... Summarizing, the project may seem successful if the time/budget constraints have been met, but the system may still be an overall failure or vice versa. So these conventional measures of project success are only partial and possibly misleading measures when taken in isolation (Shenhar and Levy, 1997)."*
>
> — A Framework of ERP Systems Implementation
> Success in China: An Empirical Study

Whether a project meets its deadlines is a completely different measurement from whether a project is successful. Let's take the analogy of building a house. A house can be built even faster than its predicted project plan. However it can be built with a variety of leaks in the roof, which only become apparent after the buyer has moved in. Beating deadlines is a nice side benefit, but the primary benefit is a **well-implemented system**. Unfortunately, whether something like a software implementation is successful is much more difficult to determine than a poorly constructed house. Some systems can simply fail to accept new users—the Healthcare.gov website being one of the most famous recent examples of this problem. However, most system problems or shortcomings are much more subtle than this. Systems may seem to operate properly, but only experienced analysis by those with the domain expertise can say for sure if the output of the system is correct. I have personally analyzed systems that were performing very poorly, but the client was not aware of this fact.

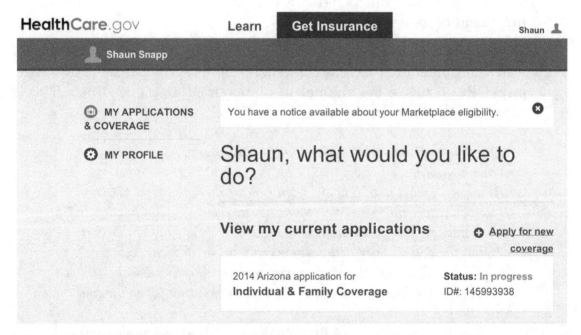

When millions of individuals signed up for health care through the healthcare.gov website, they were told that the site was not operating properly. When I signed up I received a permanent "In Progress" status for weeks.

That the HealthCare.gov site did not allow individuals to sign up was a clear sign of failure. However, this actually meant that the project missed its deadline. It does not mean that the website will **not** be a success (after I wrote this initially, it was widely reported that the website's performance had improved substantially). On the other hand, if the site had been functional, allowing people to sign up, but had resulted in worse or more expensive coverage than they had been able to access previously, then this would have been a more serious failure. If that had been the case, success or failure would have been more difficult to determine because the output would have required analysis. Actually, HealthCare.gov did result in higher premiums for many people who bought their own insurance, but this was not related to the logic of the site (when the website was finally available). Instead higher premiums were due to the fact that the regulations of the Affordable Health Care Act essentially raised the bar on what type of insurance could be purchased, placing restrictions on what were clear abuses by insurance companies. This topic brings up a litany of complexities and different viewpoints as to price changes, which I believe makes the point regarding the complexity involved in measuring success. Clearly, a website that provides no output at all is easier to recognize as a failure and not a success.

Conclusion

Enterprise software implementation success estimation is contextual. There are many factors that enter into a determination of whether a software implementation worked out for a company. Most of the time, companies don't know if their implementations were successful, because they lack the methods and willingness to invest in measurement. However, enterprise software project failure is a common and ever looming risk. The high failure rate of enterprise software projects should cause buyers to take serious precautions to improve the likelihood of success, just as most people do when faced with a risky endeavor. In other areas of life, such as in vehicle safety, we take important precautions that are universally supported as ideas, such as wearing seatbelts, bicycle helmets, etc. However, the difference in enterprise software is that there are multiple entities promoting riskier implementation behavior, and actively attempting to minimize the interpretation of risk on the part of the buyer—which is prominently the consulting companies and software vendors. However, the desire to access desirable functionality and "improve the business" can make individuals internal to buyers also push for risky implementations.

CHAPTER 4

Understanding the Enterprise Software Market

Any selection of enterprise software happens within the context of the enterprise software market. Most people who write about the enterprise software market either depend upon it for their livelihood or write about the entities that happen to be major advertisers in their publication; these writers do not have an incentive to describe how it really works.[7]

In the academic world, the **Economics** department would be well-suited to analyzing the enterprise software, but economists have little interest in studying how the enterprise software market works. I have performed the research, and there are very few articles or papers written by economists about the enterprise software market, which is both strange and quite unfortunate. A substantial portion of the improvement in productivity (something that economists are quite interested in) is due to enterprise software. It also means that anticompetitive behavior, which reduces the efficiency of the enterprise software market, is not called out, because those most qualified to write on the topic

---

[7] Please see the SCM Focus Press book, *Gartner and the Magic Quadrant: A Guide for Buyers, Vendors and Investors.*

and to compare and contrast the enterprise software market with other sectors of the economy are not part of the conversation.[8]

I have written SCM Focus articles that go so far as to analyze the enterprise software market, and these are available at the link below:

http://www.scmfocus.com/enterprisesoftwarepolicy

Although I am not an economist, in writing these articles I applied principles of economics such as tests for market efficiency, anticompetitive techniques used by certain vendors, and the industry's interaction with consulting firms and other actors. I used some of these articles in writing this book, as the nature of the enterprise software market is such that it determines what is available for a buyer to choose from during a software selection. It is critical to understand this before making a software selection.

Background on the Enterprise Software Market

Before we discuss the particulars of enterprise software market efficiency, let's cover some of the general requirements of an efficient market. It is important that one know what an efficient market looks like before one can evaluate the efficiency of a currently existing market such as enterprise software.

Requirements for an Efficient Market

1. *Prices are Published and Easily Compared:* To have an efficient market, buyers must be able to perform price comparisons. If one looks on Amazon for laptops, it is easy to perform price comparisons. Buyers drive more volume to lower cost providers, making the providers search for more ways to be efficient. Producers have a natural inclination to hide prices, meaning that the buyer must spend more time determining pricing information and less price transparency makes it more likely that the buyer will overpay.

---

[8] In fact, economists so rarely comment on technology that it was jarring to find an article on "The Decline of E-Empires" by Paul Krugman, one of the most prominent economists in the US. http://www.scmfocus.com/enterprisesoftwarepolicy/2012/03/11/why-the-largest-enterprise-software-companies-have-no-reason-to-innovate/

2. *The Product Is Easily Compared or Rated by **Unbiased** Third Parties:* If buyers do not know what they are buying and cannot differentiate between products, it is very difficult for an efficient market to exist. For instance, agricultural commodities tend to have efficient markets because an ounce of gold or soybeans is considered the same thing regardless of who is selling. Of course few items can match the comparability of agricultural commodities. *Consumer Reports* assists greatly in rating products and services for the consumer market and uses objective criteria in order to provide ratings. However, not all consumers **use** *Consumer Reports* to make decisions, and many instead follow marketing messages and salesmanship, or allow retailers (who are not objective sources of information; they have a bias) to steer them into purchases. Amazon.com also provides consumers with the ability to compare products through the use of reviews (although there are a suspicious number of books with 4.5 star average reviews). However, these types of information tools are far less available in the business-to-business market, which is a major reason IT consultancies have so much power.

3. *Producers Must Be Regulated:* Efficient markets normally require regulation. This is because producers will often purchase their competitors in order to eliminate a competitor in the marketplace and gain an unfair advantage. With a competitor eliminated, the producer can then raise their prices and reduce investment into their product. This is the strategy of all the serial acquirers in enterprise software. In fact, raising the price and reducing investment are two of the most common outcomes of software acquisitions. If the producers are not regulated, it is very similar to a competitive sport game without any referees; there is simply no incentive to not cheat. Regulating markets protects the market, but not the producers in the market. The concept of regulation is to make the markets work for the **most** individuals. Those who oppose regulation often oppose it on grounds that the regulation restricts freedom, but this is incorrect because unregulated markets are not at all "free." The result of unregulated markets is tyranny by what eventually become monopolistic producers. This hurts not only the consumers, but also other producers who are marginalized or eliminated from the market by the large monopolistic producers. This is not simply conjecture, but can be quite easily demonstrated through the evaluation of any industrial sector that has insufficient regulation.

4. *Sellers Must Have Low Monopoly Power:* A monopoly is technically a single seller with multiple buyers. However, this is a relatively rare scenario, and economists have broadened out the term to mean "tending toward" monopoly, as was described earlier in this book. Some types of production are so efficient when produced in a large scale—such as power generation—that they tend toward having only one seller. These are referred to as natural monopolies and normally are highly regulated.[9] Wherever unregulated monopolies exist, customer service/satisfaction/innovation declines and prices increase. This is one reason why the large software vendors are so poor at innovation. Sellers generally only innovate if they need to compete, and many companies that say they are innovative are not innovative in the least. Declarations of innovation are constant, predictable and are often used to justify high profits, which are due not to innovation but to a monopolistic position in the market. This is explained with regard to software vendors in the following article.

> http://www.scmfocus.com/enterprisesoftwarepolicy/2012/03/11/
> why-the-largest-enterprise-software-companies-have-no-reason-
> to-innovate/

Now that we have set the requirements for an efficient market, let us see how the enterprise software market compares.

How Enterprise Software Stacks Up

Are Prices Published and Easily Compared?

There is not a single answer to this question as it varies depending upon the software vendor. In general, prices are not published in enterprise software. The

---

[9] Without regulation of a natural monopoly, the monopolist could charge extremely high rates. A perfect example of this scenario was Enron. The energy market in California was deregulated under the Pete Wilson administration. Not surprisingly, Enron and other energy trading firms were instrumental in lobbying to have deregulation passed. Enron's traders created shortages of power specifically so they could massively increase the price of power. They did this in a state at a time when their energy generating capacity was one third higher than energy demand. Enron did everything from move power out of the state to call utilities and tell them to make up an excuse to go down for maintenance during peak periods. Enron then charged many times the standard cost of the energy. While a kilowatt-hour may have normally traded for $35, with $40 being a high price, Enron would charge $1,000 per kilowatt-hour. This is what happens when an unregulated monopoly is allowed to run wild. It results in price gouging.

software vendors that publish their prices tend to be the **low cost producers**. For instance the two software vendors Demand Works and Arena Solutions—being the low- or lower-cost producers in their respective software categories—publish their prices right on their website. Salesforce.com does the same, but is not actually the low-cost producer; a special feature of the CRM software category is that it is particularly transparent. CRM is an interesting case study as a software category as the software costs are remarkably close to one another. For instance SAP, which follows a high-cost strategy for most of its other applications does **not** follow this strategy in the CRM market, and SAP CRM is about the same price as many other applications in the CRM category. CRM also has the most SaaS offerings, which appears to be an impetus to more price transparency.

Complicated Pricing

In the enterprise software market, pricing is complicated. Pricing is based partially upon how many users will be on the system; a user is called a "seat." However, a host of other factors also come into play, including extra add-ons. For instance, beyond different levels of usage, there are add-on modules or integration modules that have a separate price. Another factor is how strategic the account is considered to be to the software company; if they think they can gain a big bump in credibility from selling to one particular client, the price may come down. Instead, prices are given only after **considerable interaction** between the vendor and the company. SAP and Oracle, being the high cost producers, rarely publish their prices. For instance, SAP publishes the price of Crystal Reports—advertising it in effect—but Crystal Reports is their lowest cost application (although it is not a low-cost application in terms of its TCO). They do not publish pricing information for most of the SAP product line, which typically is the most expensive in any category. Publishing prices only where you are competitive is not pricing transparency—in fact it is misleading. In general, most software vendors do not publish their prices. Furthermore, many vendors treat requests for pricing information as opportunities to **gain information** in order to make a sale. Often the salespeople at software vendors will continually ask for more interactions and more information in order to "meet your special needs." They have a series of rationales based on ostensible dedication to quality, which interfere with any entity that wants to determine pricing. They make statements such as, "We don't like to just throw out pricing numbers without knowing the situation."

Of course, the software vendors could make their pricing much more simple, so determining price would not require such extensive information. At Software Decisions our *Product Planning Package,* as well as our *TCO Calculator,* estimates software costs based upon variable user input; if software companies wanted to, they could put similar calculators on their websites. However, most choose not to do this. In fact, software vendors often seem to go out of their way to make their software difficult to compare with alternatives. As a result, it takes a **great deal** of effort to determine pricing, at least with many, if not most, vendors.

Call us at +1 484-653-5345

Solutions | Products | Services | Try & Buy | Info | Contact

SMOOTHIE PRICING

Smoothie® by Demand Works is available in standalone or server-based configurations as well as different editions to satisfy a range of demand and supply planning needs. See the Products and Solutions sections for more information about the various Smoothie editions, or contact Demand Works for a quote or specific configuration advice.

Smoothie Power User Pricing (Standalone or Server)

	Base Price*	Price With Required 1-Yr Maintenance*
Smoothie Learning Edition	$500	N/A**
Smoothie Plus	$4,000	$4,800
Smoothie SP	$5,000	$6,000
Spreadsheet Collaboration Add-On (for Smoothie Plus or Smoothie SP Users only. Individual collaborator user licenses are available for Smoothie Mambo.)	$2,500	$3,000

Server-Based Configurations

Various user types are available with server configurations including read-only users, collaborators, and power users. Smoothie Plus is the license type for demand power users, and Smoothie SP user licenses are required for supply & demand planners (see standalone pricing, above). Collaborator users can review, annotate and adjust forecast but they can not change statistical forecast settings, manage imports or work with Pivot Maps®. Read-Only users can review any Smoothie data or plans plans but they can't modify them in any way. An alternative spreadsheet-based user interface can be used for collaborators as well.

Below are some sample configurations for team-based demand, or supply and demand planning. The pricing examples below include first year

It does not get much easier in terms of pricing than Demand Works.

Server-Based Configurations

Various user types are available with server configurations including read-only users, collaborators, and power users. Smoothie Plus is the license type for demand power users, and Smoothie SP user licenses are required for supply & demand planners (see standalone pricing, above). Collaborator users can review, annotate and adjust forecast but they can not change statistical forecast settings, manage imports or work with Pivot Maps®. Read-Only users can review any Smoothie data or plans plans but they can't modify them in any way. An alternative spreadsheet-based user interface can be used for collaborators as well.

Below are some sample configurations for team-based demand, or supply and demand planning. The pricing examples below include first year maintenance and multi-user bracket discounts. Contact Demand Works for a written estimate based on your specific configuration.

	Price (Incl. Required 1st Yr. Maintenance)
Small Demand Planning Team (Smoothie Mambo Server, 1 Demand Planner, 10 Collaborator Users)	$24,900
Five Buyer-Planners with Read-Only Users (Smoothie Mambo Server, 5 Supply Planners, 5 Read-Only Users)	$33,600

Cloud-Based Configurations

Like Smoothie Mambo, Cloud Smoothie pricing is calculated based on the number of licensed users of each type. However, it is offered as a monthly subscription instead of as a one-time perpetual license charge. Please complete the contact form for a free consultation and pricing.

Smoothie Integration Connectors

Demand Works offers pre-built integrations for various ERP platforms including Microsoft Dynamics AX, Dynamics NAV, and Dynamics GP, as well as the SYSPRO ERP platform. The Smoothie integration connectors significantly reduce the amount of initial and ongoing integration effort and they are priced at $3,000 per server, excluding required maintenance.

* All prices are per Named User except for Smoothie Mambo which is licensed per production server. See EULA for licensing details. **Required first-year annual maintenance is 20% of net license cost per year for all products except Smoothie Learning Edition.** All prices are subject to change without notice.

** Maintenance is not available for Smoothie Learning Edition. Limit one per company.

*** Smoothie Mambo software is licensed per production server. One server may contain several models and be used by several groups of users within a given enterprise. There is no additional charge for additional instances for backup, QA or testing purposes.

Contact Demand Works for full pricing information or demonstrations. Follow this link to learn everything there is to know about how to try and buy Smoothie.

However, a number of different factors must be added up before arriving at the correct price. The pricing listed here is meant to prompt the customer to call for more explanation.

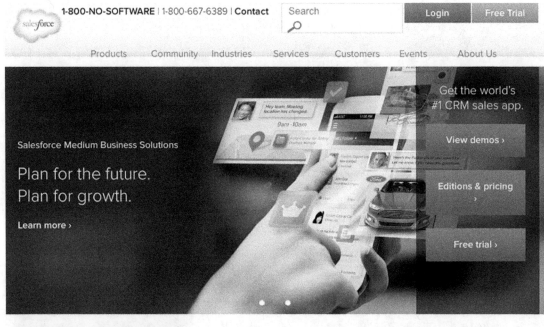

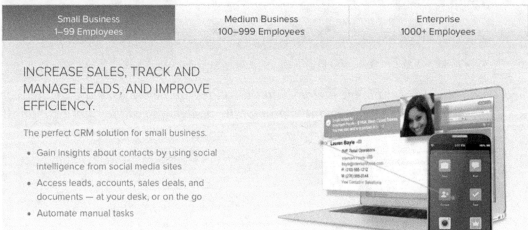

Salesforce was one of the first vendors to provide a great deal of transparency to prospects right on their website. Salesforce provides options for getting details about their application right on the first page. Salesforce will allow anyone to get into their demo system immediately.

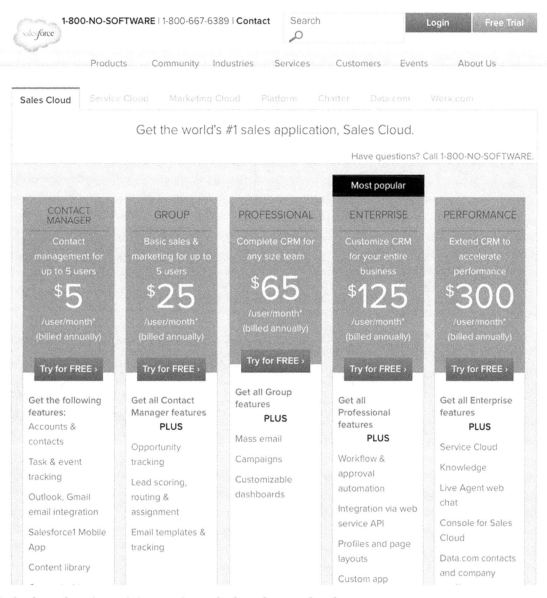

Salesforce has its pricing options declared very clearly.

Inexpensive or even free trials help clients. Salesforce offers very inexpensive lower-level CRM functionality, allowing the buyer to test drive the application before they commit to much of anything.

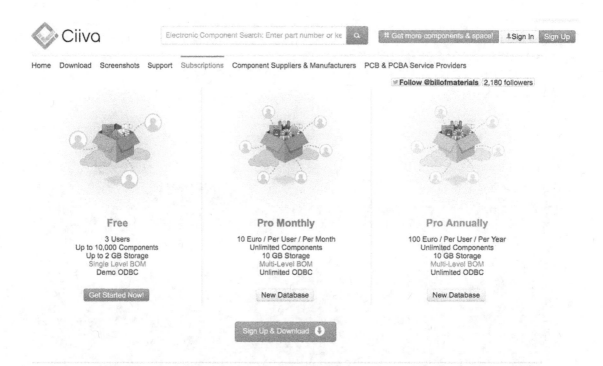

Software vendors like Ciiva provide free versions of their applications that prospects can use for as long as they like. For more fully functional versions of the software, the prospect is migrated to paid versions. As applications become more SaaS-based (something that is inevitable), we see this model becoming more common.

However, the more monopolistic the vendor, the less pricing information they make available. Oracle's prices are nothing to brag about, and therefore essentially you can't find published pricing information at the Oracle website. In fact, you can't find demos or videos of Oracle on their site either (although you can find them on YouTube). The Oracle website is all about getting prospects to contact Oracle directly.

The Elusiveness of Total Costs

Often software costs are not published, and when they are, considerable interpretation is required to come to the final software costs. However, these are not the total costs that the company will pay for use of the application. For the applications we have priced at Software Decisions, the software cost averages a little less than 10 percent of the total cost of ownership (TCO) of the application, and the proportion of the overall costs vary.[10] The largest cost by far is maintenance costs. The graphic below shows the average breakdown per the software categories that we track, of the applications we have analyzed.

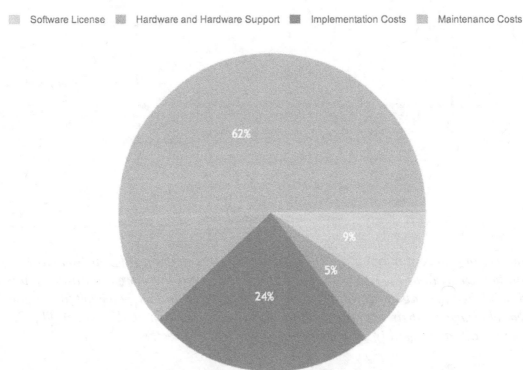

Enterprise Software Costs (TCO) by Cateogry

Software License ■ Hardware and Hardware Support ■ Implementation Costs ■ Maintenance Costs

We are constantly adding to our application database, so these percentages will change over time. However, these are reliable figures to use for estimation of enterprise software costs, although they do vary per application. This graphic only displays the average cost.

---

[10] This website can be found at http://www.softwaredecisions.com

The rare buyer or software vendor that performs a TCO analysis will often **leave out** many costs. This is why I refer to almost every TCO study that I reviewed for the book *Enterprise Software TCO: Calculating and Using Total Cost of Ownership for Decision Making*, as a "partial cost of ownership" study, or a "PCO." The TCO analysis at Software Decisions estimates costs of internal implementation (that is the cost of internal resources assigned to the project) as well as internal support costs on the business side.

Most buyers make purchasing decisions that are based substantially upon the **initial** cost—the software license cost—rather than the TCO. In fact, estimation of TCO, in any substantial way, is exceedingly rare. I find this strange, because there are **so** many white papers on the importance of selecting applications with a low TCO. However, talking about low TCO and actually producing a low TCO are two completely different things. Most entities in the enterprise software space say simply that TCO is "important, but unknowable."

With multiple factors complicating the calculation of costs, costs are frequently unknown in the enterprise software market. This makes decision-making more difficult for enterprise software buyers and works against market efficiency.

Can the Product Be Easily Compared or Rated by Unbiased Third Parties?

The subsection deals with how buyers interpret the products in the market and how easy or how difficult it is to understand the features and value of the product.

Ease of Product Comparison

Enterprise software cannot be compared easily. One's interpretation of this complex product changes depending upon perspective, the source of the product information, and what pre-existing software the buyer has purchased. Frequently, enterprise software buyers will not understand much about what they are buying. This is simply the nature of enterprise software, which is one of the most complex products that any company will purchase.

Enterprise software is, in fact, far more complex than computer hardware. Understanding computer hardware at a detailed level means understanding physics, particularly how electrons are controlled by various mechanisms. However, it is not necessary to get to that level of detail to make purchase decisions, as computer hardware specifications can be compared. Software **cannot** be compared as easily based on gross specifications. It can take years of working with an application to appreciate the distinctions between various applications. As an example, I had worked with PlanetTogether's Galaxy APS for at least three years before I realized it contained multi-plant planning functionality, and I did not realize this until I met this business requirement for a client. Except in software categories such as CRM, it is simply impossible to know everything about what an enterprise software application can do, and how it can be used.

The main way in which buyers become familiar with enterprise software applications in any detail is through software demonstrations. Most demonstrations or demos are performed through site visits or—increasingly—through screen sharing during web conference sessions. Some software vendors provide potential customers with online access to demonstration systems, but most software vendors do not offer this option. Many software vendors make the argument that their applications are too complex for prospects to understand through an online demonstration system, and there is some merit to this argument. However, a few hours spent with a person who is an expert in an application is nowhere near enough time to understand an enterprise software application.

Third Party Ratings

Consumer Reports is an excellent example of a financially independent entity that provides product and vendor ratings and is a great boon to the efficiency of the market for consumer products. Yelp is another example of a rating entity. While they cannot police every fake review written, it is not known to have a financial bias toward those entities that are rated. That is, a local dentist cannot pay Yelp to change its reviews. Yelp has been extremely important in improving the efficiency of the market for local services, channeling more customers to higher-rated businesses—which improves market efficiency.

Few financially unbiased media entities exist that **provide objective information** on enterprise software. Through interviews with buyers, as well as by troubleshooting and diagnosing problematic implementations, a picture emerges of buyers who **are not able to** determine application capabilities, level of vendor innovation, or even the fit between enterprise software and their business requirements. It is no accident that the applications that score best in our multiple dimensions—specifically for maintainability, usability, functionality and implement-ability (what we call MUFI for short)—rarely include the best-selling applications in their respective software categories.

The Santa Claus Syndrome

Unlike the consumer software market, the executives who make the purchasing decisions are never the same as those people who actually **use** the software. At Software Decisions we refer to this as the Santa Claus Syndrome; just as with Christmas, when the buyer is buying for someone else, the gift is not as good a fit as if the recipient bought for himself.

http://www.scmfocus.com/softwaredecisions/santa-clause-syndrome/

The purchasing outcomes—even when the buyer places the interests of the recipient above those of the seller—are almost always inferior to when the individuals (who must use and live with the selection) make the selection themselves.[11]

In most cases, neither the executives nor anyone else at the company will use the solution prior to the purchase. Typically the potential customer will see several software demonstrations or review some screen shots. Much of what is published about the software in marketing literature—or what vendor salespeople talk about—is of limited accuracy or is not applicable to an actual implementation.

---

[11] In fact, there are many cases where those responsible for corporate purchases place the seller's interests ahead of the recipients, such as in cases where the decision maker is being compensated in some shape or form by the seller. Compensation can come in many forms, such as seller-provided dinners and gifts. Sellers provide these enticements precisely because they move the decision-making away from the actual attributes of the purchased item. This practice extends from the corporate procurement environment to the government procurement environment (where political donations overwhelmingly control contracts) and to doctors' offices, where in most cases doctors will write prescriptions for patented drugs that often have either very similar or identical chemical properties to a drug for which there is a generic option. Because of this *Consumer Reports* recommends always asking doctors, "is another less expensive drug that can be substituted for this drug you are recommending?" The pharmaceutical companies compensate the doctor to offer "free samples" of the patented drug to promote the continual purchase and use of the drug. Patients who choose patent alternatives, in the US at least, must ask the doctor if it exists, but most patients don't do this.

Not understanding the distinctions between the applications themselves, corporate decision-makers rely upon sales representatives, consulting companies, and IT analyst firms for this information, and each of these entities have their own financial incentives. Not only are these incentives misaligned, but they are aligned against their client's interests.

Are Producers Regulated?

Enterprise software is not consumed orally, and it can't hurt anyone physically. Thus, the main form of regulation to protect buyers and create an efficient market would be to regulate the messages sent out by software vendors—ensure that the messages are true and that statements related to functionality (in user manuals and release notes) are also true.

Regulation of Statements by Software Vendors

As anyone who has worked in enterprise software can tell you, there is no restriction on what software companies can say. Any software company can make any announcement it likes regardless of how false that statement might be, and no government agency will come knocking on the company's door asking for a retraction. And it's worse than false information and puffery in marketing documentation; some of the information in release notes describes functionality that either does not work or does not work as intended. There is no regulation of what software vendors say or write in their documentation. The government seems to have problems regulating food labels; regulating software for accuracy of the "contents" would be far more complicated than regulating food labels, as software is more complicated and more subjective.

Regulation of the Concentration of Market Power

Most enterprise software companies originate and are based in the US. It is extremely rare for software acquisitions to be disallowed by the Federal Trade Commission (FTC), even in cases where it is quite clear that the acquisition increased monopoly power (e.g., the all too obvious Oracle acquisition of PeopleSoft). The effect of software acquisitions is to restrict choice, increase prices and allow large and inefficient software vendors that are poor at innovation to continually replenish their application base with new applications. It also increases risk for buyers substantially. A buyer can make an intelligent purchasing decision; find an easy to work with smaller software vendor with a great application. However, at any time that smaller, high-value, innovative vendor can be acquired, and a buyer can find himself or herself sitting across from major software vendors (i.e., "sharks") and the value proposition can turn upside down very quickly. The customers of Business Objects found out about this when SAP radically reduced the service support for Business Objects after the acquisition. The support was so poor that it became the subject of articles in the mainstream IT press.

If software acquisitions were not allowed, the larger vendors would eventually give way to the smaller and more innovative vendors. For instance, a primary reason as to why SAP purchased Business Objects and why Oracle purchased PeopleSoft is that these software vendors were **beating** SAP and Oracle in competitions, and this was just "too much competition" for these two entities. Most likely SAP and Oracle would have continued to lose market share to these vendors.

The standard applied by the FTC for acquisition approval is where the combined entity would increase market concentration on what is referred to as the Herfindahl Index. I won't go into the Herfindahl Index, but essentially it is a way to justify any acquisition or merger based upon esoteric criteria that has little to do with the practical outcomes of mergers. The entire exercise is academic, because most of the FTC employees that have decision-making ability are part of the revolving door between industry and government and worked for the industry they regulate, and will return to industry after their stint at the FTC. The FTC has been fully captured and only in very extraordinary instances does it look out for anyone's interests aside from the major enterprise software producers.

Enterprise software mergers and acquisitions are a major way for uncompetitive vendors to stay relevant and in control of the market, and *the* primary way to maintain their monopolistic power.

Sellers Must Not Have Monopoly Power

Typically, the fact that the biggest software vendors have monopoly power in the enterprise software market is **not discussed**. While the concept of competition existed at one time—as is evidenced by anti-trust legislation like the Sherman and the Clayton anti-trust acts—the idea that companies should have to follow any rules of competition or that the government has a role in keeping markets efficient has faded in the US culture.

Why the Enterprise Software Market Is Inefficient

Monopoly power exists in the enterprise software market for the simple reason that there is little to no incentive to keep the market for enterprise software competitive. Although many would like to propose it, there is no "natural" reason for this. Some would make the argument that noncompetition is simply *"the way of the market."* However, it isn't. Instead the lack of competition is because of how the game is set up. Furthermore, the present inefficient state of the enterprise software market is quite good evidence (although no further evidence is really required on this point) that markets left to their own devices result in inefficient outcomes. The deck is stacked against buyers and the likelihood of overpaying and ending up with an underperforming system is quite high; in fact, it happens quite frequently, and it shows up in the success/failure statistics. The underlying reasons for why this happens are not illuminated or are poorly illuminated by IT media entities, which must be careful not to alienate advertisers and other funding sources. It is not much of a logical leap to understand that buyers in this market face a much higher risk than if the market were regulated.

If consulting companies were not allowed to sell implementation services to the same clients they advise, the market power of the largest software companies would be seriously compromised. If mergers were disallowed, within a decade the structure of the enterprise software market would be significantly changed for the better.

The Outcome of an Efficient and Inefficient Market

Let's go over whose interests are served in an efficient market versus an inefficient market.

1. *Consumers:* An efficient market serves consumers.

2. *Prices:* An efficient market produces lower prices.

3. *Producers:* An inefficient market serves some privileged producers, but **not all** producers. An inefficient market works against the high-quality producers/software vendors that do not have monopoly power, and works

for producers that have monopoly power and prefer to provide poor value to their customers.

4. *Workers:* Workers benefit by working for employers that have monopoly power. In the enterprise software area, employees that work for Microsoft, SAP and Oracle are paid well versus their counterparts working for companies that do not have monopoly power. In fact, unions tend to unionize companies that have monopoly power and tend to stay away from companies that lack this power. Companies with monopoly power make excess profits because of this power, and some of this excess profit is shared with workers. Workers for monopoly companies are quick to assume that the company they work for is the "best" rather than acknowledge that the company is controlling the market through unfair competition.

5. *Innovation:* Usually innovation is reduced in monopolistic conditions. The major monopolistic software vendors (Microsoft, SAP, IBM and Oracle) are better known for **buying or copying** innovation rather than creating innovation. SAP's primary innovation was its ERP system, which was developed decades ago when they did not have the monopoly power that they do today.[12] Initially Oracle was innovative in databases, but again that was earlier in the company's history. Most of their recent activity has simply been buying other software vendors in order to increase their monopoly power.[13] This change in innovation level over time is why Software Decisions rates

---

[12] SAP actively reverse-engineers software from other software vendors. They actually had a program that was nothing more than an enormous competitive intelligence gathering program cloaked as a partnership program.

http://www.scmfocus.com/inventoryoptimizationmultiechelon/2010/01/its-time-for-the-sap-xapps-program-to-die/, http://www.scmfocus.com/enterprisesoftwarepolicy/2012/01/27/how-common-is-it-for-sap-to-take-intellectual-property-from-partners/.

SAP lost a case to Oracle for downloading enormous amounts of its intellectual property through SAP's TomorrowNow subsidiary.

[13] The counterexample of the relationship between monopoly and innovation is that two of the most important private research laboratories of the twentieth century were Bell Labs (funded by the AT&T monopoly) and PARC (funded by the Xerox monopoly). But in general, innovation declines as monopoly power increases. Apple has been enormously innovative, actually serving as the R&D entity for the computing industry. Many computer and software companies don't seem to do much innovation themselves, but simply reverse-engineer whatever Apple comes up with. It will be interesting to see if Apple continues to innovate as it becomes a monopoly power.

a vendor's Current Innovation Level. The current innovation level is a far better predictor of future innovation than past innovation.

http://www.scmfocus.com/softwaredecisions/current-innovation-level/

With an efficient market, more often than not, customers receive good value for their purchases and don't have much of a problem finding the best product for their needs. Over the long term, in the absence of regulation, markets tend toward monopoly rather than perfect competition, as is often proposed by those promoting free markets. Those who propose the markets will move towards perfect competition or efficiency without regulation tend to be either monopolists or media outlets funded by monopolists.

Making Better Decisions in the Future

It is important to understand that much of the information necessary to make good software selection decisions in the enterprise software market is hidden from view and difficult to obtain. In most cases, you must contact each vendor directly to obtain this information. You must also interact with them and go through their process (which they control).

I have painted a rather bleak picture; however, in many ways the future looks brighter. Several changes are underway that buyers will be able to leverage to improve their chances of obtaining better outcomes:

SaaS applications: The CRM software category provides support for the theory that online and hosted applications would naturally lead to a more efficient market for enterprise software. Not only are SaaS-based solutions more transparent in areas ranging from pricing to the ability of buyers to experience enterprise software first-hand, but SaaS solutions have a much lower TCO, go live more quickly, and have much less lock-in than on-premises solutions. SaaS software vendors must be more concerned with the satisfaction of their customer base than on-premises vendors—and most of them know this. Arena Solutions sells their SaaS solution to most of their customers, although they do offer an on-premises version. Arena Solutions knows that their success is dependent greatly upon repeat user subscriptions, and they state their belief openly that the SaaS model aligns the interests of the software vendor with their clients' interests more tightly.

Crowdsourcing Websites: A second positive feature of the enterprise software market is the rise of crowdsourcing websites that democratize the review and rating of applications. In my book *Gartner and the Magic Quadrant: A Guide for Buyers, Vendors and Investors*, I was openly skeptical whether a crowdsourcing website could replace Gartner, and for many executive decision-makers, I think this is true. However, I have much more faith in the objectivity and validity of application ratings in a site like G2 Crowd than I do in Gartner. Secondly, the level of coverage Gartner provides about an application is far too high, and I believe many other IT analysts make this same mistake. High-level information is bad for decision making. The most important feature of purchasing any application is **not** the high-level strategic considerations highlighted by Gartner and many other IT analysts, as any application can be made to work with the current applications that are in-house. Instead, the best determinant of whether an application will be a good fit for a company is whether it meets its business requirements. Gartner and many other IT analysts have gotten away from this truth, and it has led to poor outcomes for those who have taken this advice.

Buyers need to stop listening to entities with a financial bias, and start leveraging SaaS applications and more democratic forms of application reviews and ratings. The good news is that because of these developments, it is quite possible for buyers to make much better decisions regarding the purchase of enterprise software.

Conclusion

The enterprise software market is almost entirely **unregulated**. Economists pay little attention to the market, and most people who write about the enterprise software market either depend upon it for their livelihood or write about the entities that happen to be major advertisers in their publication; these writers do not have an incentive to describe how it really works. This chapter brought up the common requirements for an efficient market, and found that the enterprise software market is lacking in all of them. This is what happens when a market is unregulated, and also makes enterprise software selection and risk management much more difficult.

CHAPTER 5

Software Sell-ability versus Implement-ability

In many parts of this book I explain how to make the software selection more about implement-ability rather than the sell-ability of the software. The reader will also understand why the marketing literature reads the way it does and why they need to ignore the "sell-ability" parts of it and seek instead documentation that reflects the "implement-ability" of the software. They will better understand the types of questions they need to ask of references, and check whether they consider the reference to be one the company provided merely to add to their "sell-ability." By understanding the difference between sell-ability and implement-ability, it's easier to understand where the real interest lies for the entities that provide information to the selection process.

Many pressures cause software to be developed into what you see as the final product. This information sets the stage for the end of the chapter, which will focus on how to select the most implementable solution. It would, of course, be quite nice if software were always designed to be functional rather than sold. Vendors have a limited amount of resources that they can apply to the development of their products.

There is a general misimpression that software development occurs along the lines of what is desired by customers, which should lead to desirable outcomes. This sounds plausible enough. However, the reality of software development (and this applies to all enterprise software to varying degrees) is that there are competing agendas: not only the customers' agenda but also the vendor's and even those of third parties such as IT analyst firms. This problem is exacerbated at the larger software vendors where the strongest incentives exist to throw things over the wall. I recall having a discussion on this topic with representatives from the vendor PlanetTogether. I asked them why their software seemed so much more usable than other software in their software category, and one example they gave was that the company was just too small to throw things over walls and develop functionality that had little practical implementation value just to get a sale. The smaller the entity, the more affiliation each individual has with other individuals, the more they personally know them—can receive negative feedback for aggressively perusing one's personal agenda at the expense of others.

So far I have only explained the agendas internal to the vendor, however it does not end there. As will be explained in Chapter 7: "How to Use the Reports of Analyst Firms Like Gartner," because vendors want to score well in IT analyst ratings, they are under pressure to match the vision that the IT analysts have for their software category. The same issue applies for software investors. Software investors have a particular story that they find more appealing for investing. For instance, Adobe is well-known for its suite of design applications that includes Photoshop and Illustrator. However, Adobe decided to move to a SaaS-based solution, which meant that users now rent the Adobe creative products for a monthly fee. While there were several reasons for this change, one stated reason was to stabilize the company's revenues (moving to a monthly charge rather than seeing its revenue bunched up after their upgrades are released), thus making Adobe more appealing to stock analysts who prefer to see stable revenues. However, was this the best-combined solution if customer's interests were accounted for? Many people that use Adobe's creative products don't think so.

Even if we limit our discussion to just the vendor and buyer, there are multiple people in multiple departments who often have competing objectives. If we take just the vendor's competing objectives, for instance, one of the pressures comes from the need to have implementable software that buyers can actually use. However, other pressures come from the need to sell software. The agendas of those who sell software and make software implementable may sound complementary, but in fact they are not at all complementary and are a major source of friction within vendors.

The Case Study of i2 Technologies

I once worked for a software company called i2 Technologies, which is a textbook example of what happens when marketing and sales completely co-opt product development. Not only did i2 Technologies come out with too many new product enhancements, they simply came out with too many new products. I2 Technologies fell victim to Enron Syndrome—too much confidence in one's innovation, too much focus on the stock price rather than the business, and accounting irregularities (necessary in order to keep continual improvements in earnings). Most of i2's best products were the first ones they developed, before the media created an echo chamber for them and Enron Syndrome took hold. I found out first hand as a consultant implementing projects the new products were universally the problem applications. Few of these products actually worked and it eventually brought down i2 Technologies, once a thought leader in its space. The company was acquired cheaply by JDA. I worked in consulting within i2 Technologies, and there was a great deal of friction between marketing/sales and consulting because we were not able to deliver reference-able accounts because the new software was essentially not implementable.

Functionality Creep

An important component of how companies rate software is how many areas of functionality the software includes, which in turn encourages vendors to add more and more functionality. However, this continually-added functionality also increases maintenance and quality problems. That is, it is easy for a software vendor to bring out more functionality than it can reasonably maintain. Vendors do this because Marketing and Sales repeatedly go to Development and say, *"If we only had this area of functionality we would get this big client."* Buyers who have already purchased software constantly ask vendors for adjustments to the software, and in most cases they are not willing to pay for these improvements but simply want them rolled into the next version of the software. However, buyers have a self-centered view of the software, only seeing the things ***they want to do*** in the software. Generally, they do not understand the vision of the software, and are mostly unconcerned as to whether or not other buyers are also interested in using the software in the same manner. In essence, clients would like to turn a software vendor into their personal custom-development shop, while vendors need to make sure that the functionality they develop can be sold to multiple clients. Sales and Marketing know what they can sell, but are frequently inconsiderate of how adding new functionality can negatively impact the maintainability of an application. Therefore, the buyer, sales and marketing, with their focus on adding functionality, have a much more limited view of the software product than does Product Management.

The product management process maintains this list of product enhancements (some driven by customers, some internally driven, some driven by sales), estimates how much the enhancements will take in terms of time and money, and prioritizes the enhancements that have the best potential to "improve" the software so that these are worked on first. I used the term "improve" in quotation marks because it is a subjective term. To sales, improvement means it will make the software sell better. To the buyer, it is something that will allow them to better meet their particular business requirement. To an implementation consultant, an improvement means the software will be easier to implement. To the product manager, "improve" may mean that the change is consistent with the long-term vision of the product. Therefore, the definition of the term "improve" very much depends upon who you are and your incentives and motivations.

The Dynamic Nature of Software

Software is like a living organism in that it is constantly growing and changing and has a certain life cycle. The lifespan of software is relatively short compared to other products, some reasons for which I have listed below:

1. Application software relies upon underlying layers. These layers include things like databases, operating systems and hardware. When these underlying layers change, the software must also change. For instance, if an operating system falls out of favor, the software must be ported to the new operating system. Software is designed to work on a particular category of

hardware. When the hardware changes, the software must be rewritten. For example, there has been a movement from single-processing servers to multi-processor servers. When this occurred, some vendors (particularly those who sell high performance applications) did not place porting multi-threaded processing high enough on the development prioritization list, so are still only using single processors.

2. Software is a rapidly evolving product category. Applications must be updated constantly or they become outdated. There can be classic cars—cars that you wish they still made—but classic software is really just uncompetitive software. If you were to go back and review software from a decade ago, you would notice that the software appears dated compared to current designs. In fact, much of the software we use has not been around that long, and while an application may have the same name as what was sold as the same product a decade ago, it is a very different animal.

3. Larger vendors often acquire successful and innovative small vendors. When this happens, the most common outcome is for the acquired vendor to stop being a leader in their category. The acquiring vendor simply procures the smaller vendor's customers and stops innovating with the product. Many of the employees of the acquired firm, particularly those most responsible for product innovation, leave the merged company. Acquisitions are, in fact, one of the prime causes of a software product becoming irrelevant.

4. Under constant pressure to add functionality, applications can become so high-maintenance and difficult to use that they lose their original benefit and become vulnerable to less complex products that work more efficiently. This phenomenon was recognized by the blogging platform WordPress. WordPress is the most popular blogging platform in the world, and powers many of the blogs and websites that we all read. I have been working with the software since 2007. This highly respected software is free and has grown enormously since it was originally introduced. Essentially, WordPress receives an unlimited number of requests to add functionality to its software. However, early on it decided to not develop the product to meet all of these requests, but instead to allow plug-ins. WordPress simply allows its software to interoperate with third party software vendors (most of them do

not charge for the software they create), and in this way WordPress is not responsible for developing or maintaining those plug-ins. This system has been extremely successful and has allowed WordPress to continue to grow with a seemingly unending number of plug-ins. WordPress is not distracted and instead can concentrate on what it does best, which is continuing to develop the core WordPress software. Unfortunately enterprise software does not work like this, and therefore can easily grow unwieldy under the new functionality, which results from constant requests for improvement.

Adjusting the Software Selection Approach to be Focused on Implementation

I have explained how software development and software vendors tend to work in order to help those who perform a software selection to account for these factors and to make better decisions.

The first thing that should be recognized is that the buyer will not implement all the functionality or get all of the functionality that they desire to work. A major strategy of vendors is to anticipate every need that a company could have by placing a very complete set of functionality in their applications. However, as this type of software tends to be difficult to implement, companies greatly overestimate their ability to implement functionality.

Software selections are often performed with the incorrect assumption that the buyer will place more resources on the implementation and maintenance of the implementation than they actually are willing to place. To use an example from my implementation experience, when companies select statistical forecasting applications they often are attracted to the functionality of complicated forecasting methodologies (mathematics that drive the forecast). They have much less interest in hiring and paying people with forecasting education and experience to actually run the applications. Some things can be done to simplify forecasting for individuals; however, they should be able to understand what the application is doing. Many forecasting applications have thirty different forecasting methodologies, yet at company after company I see only a few of these methodologies used. There is a way of automatically choosing among the different forecasting methodologies, and even though most companies cannot get this functionality to work, there are vendors for which this type of selection is automatic.

Secondly, there are many more practical areas of the forecasting applications that are just as important to the success of a statistical forecasting application, yet these areas are not emphasized during the software selection. One can't know what these areas are unless one was to implement and use the software oneself. This is a clear example—and just one of many examples—of how the buyer does not focus on what really matters in an implementation.

http://www.scmfocus.com/demandplanning/2010/09/why-companies-are-selecting-the-wrong-supply-chain-demand-planning-systems/

Making Realism a Priority

In the US during the past forty years, the bicycle has been transformed from a practical machine for transportation into a far less practical item that offers more ego-driven functionality (lower weight, aggressive styling, high turnover in design) and less practical functionality (ride-ability, safety, cargo capacity). The bicycle is an excellent example of the effect that marketing can have on an item's transformation. Marketing can tell a company what will sell, but they have no technical expertise to help a company understand what will work in practical usage. In fact, in most cases they undermine the design proposed by engineers or developers. If we take the example of the bicycle in the US from the perspective of usability, the redesign has been a failure. How can I say this? Well it shows up quite prominently in the distances these bikes are ridden per year. Luckily, research comparing distances ridden per country is available. Countries such as Denmark and the Netherlands are renowned for not riding US-style bikes and for retaining their older designs. A visit to Amsterdam will quickly make evident to the traveler that the styles used by the Dutch are completely different from those used in the US. The Dutch bike is known for its distinctive and traditional design. By having two countries with opposite bicycle designs and by comparing the frequency with which these bicycles are ridden, we can gain a good approximation of how effective the changes to the bicycle have been in the US.

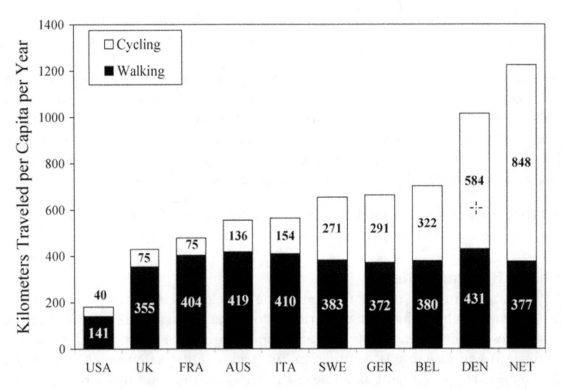

This is for the year 2000. And for that year, the average person from the Netherlands rode 21.2 times farther than the average American. In 2000 the US population was 281,421,906, while the Dutch population was 16,783,092. However, the Dutch as a country still cycled 26 percent more miles than the US.

This graphic really cannot be spun in a way that favors the US design of bikes. What is clear is that in the US, marketing influenced the design approach, which concentrates primarily on the "coolness factor" of the bicycle—that is a bike that is designed to be sold rather than ridden. This leads to a large number of bicycles that sit in the garage, not being ridden. In the US, the average bicycle is ridden forty miles per year at an average speed of just fifteen miles per hour (meaning that the average rider rides for two hours and forty minutes—over an entire year).

Furthermore it should be remembered that bicycles are a much easier "selection" decision than the selection of enterprise software. However, the transformation away from usability on these consumer items, which are tested directly before purchase, demonstrates how marketing and impracticality can affect product development.

Poor Software Selection as a Contributing Factor to the High Failure Rate of Enterprise Software Implementations

Finding the root cause for the high failure rate of enterprise software implementations has been the subject of much questioning. Poor software selection is one of the causes. In fact, while the reasons are elementary and quite easy to adjust, they will not be changed because this is simply how companies have chosen to operate and entrenched interests and ways of doing things often do not change.

Buyers are frequently more interested in factors outside of implement-ability and thus you cannot rely upon enterprise software to be designed for implement-ability. Some people have a hard time seeing why this is the case, the logic being that software that is not as implementable will eventually lose to those competitors with more implementable software. However, as I have explained earlier in this book, the enterprise software market is not an efficient market. There are many factors that drive buyer revenues, and the implement-ability of software is only one of the factors. As discussed previously, many large vendors have partnerships with large consulting companies. These large consulting companies recommend their vendor partner's software because doing so maximizes their revenues. Smaller software vendors will never enjoy this relationship with large consulting companies regardless of how implementable their software is. Software failures are hidden and the feedback loop about software's implement-ability is to a great degree broken.

Conclusion

While those in marketing will disagree, software cannot be optimized for both sales and implement-ability. Software that is highly implementable means that product management has accounted for the important enhancements but has not put every enhancement request into the product.

A major objective of the individuals who support a software selection effort is to ignore much of the marketing hyperbole and salesmanship and instead find the applications that offer the best combination of functionality to match with the buyer's requirements, while at the same time considering the implement-ability of that functionality. The buyer may not implement all of the functionality that they desire, and the implement-ability of the functionality is as important as whether or not the functionality exists in the vendor's application.

The overall theme of this chapter is that vendors have, in many ways, optimized their products to be sold rather than implemented effectively. Larger vendors are more prone to doing this than smaller vendors.

CHAPTER 6

Selecting the Right IT Consultant

Consulting companies are major influencers for enterprise software purchasing decisions. Usually, one of the major consulting companies is permanently resident as an enterprise software customer. The best place to start in understanding the advice provided by large consulting companies is to analyze their institutional structure. This tends to apply to small consulting companies as well. Understanding how consulting companies make their money is also critical to understanding how they work. As they say in political thrillers and investigative journalism, "follow the money."

There are several lines of thought regarding predicting behavior. One theory says that the individual can determine behavior of other individuals in an institution. History provides examples of this—that is, individuals who set their own agendas. However, the incentives of the institution are a more reliable guide to behavior. Individuals whose behavior diverges from the incentives of the institution tend to be short-lived in that institution. Therefore, while consulting companies are made up of a large number of people, their policy can be determined by both observing their incentives and by observing their output. Output is a far more predictive measurement than an institution's statements about itself because for the most part, an institution's behavior diverges greatly (and I mean this quite generally) from its statements. For instance, the worst thing that one could do to understand how an oil company works is to go to its website and take the statements it makes there at face value.

The Institutional Structure of Consulting Firms

Consulting companies have the following features, which are important to interpreting their advice on software selection

1. Consulting companies make their money based upon billing an hourly rate for their employees.

2. Their employees cannot be capable in all—or even a small percentage—of the software in a category. Because enterprise software is complex, ordinarily a consultant will work in both a single software vendor's application, as well as specialize in a single module within that brand. For instance, I work in SAP, which is the largest enterprise software vendor. I have worked in different modules, but I tend to get most of my work from a single module.

3. Therefore, they tend to have a deep specialization in a relatively small number of applications. Unsurprisingly, they tend to specialize in the largest applications. Specializing in a large and popular application allows a consulting company to get the highest percentage of billing hours out of their resources.

4. The people that make software recommendations to clients are called "partners." Partners are the senior management of the consulting companies. There are different levels of partners, with the most senior partners driving the policy of the consulting company. In fact, some of the policies (e.g., the policies regarding which major vendors they should focus on in their consulting practices) were decided long ago, and these policies are not decided or re-determined in any way periodically. People not familiar with the consulting market may say, "Wait a second. These consulting companies have many consultants at all different levels. Surely, when individuals work for them, a variety of viewpoints are available to consulting clients." Actually no. This is a common misconception. The consultants below the partner level have no influence on what recommendations are made. The

partner discusses what will be recommended with their consultants before meeting with the client. And this not only applies to full-time employees. When I have worked for consulting companies as an independent consultant (a so-called subcontractor) I was repeatedly pressured and told what viewpoints I should give the client. The advice I give must fit with the story that the partner wants to tell. However, they want to create the illusion that their opinion is my personal opinion. In fact, even the partners at the level I work with do not set policy. These policies, such as which software to recommend, are set far above the partners that actually work on projects, at the senior partner level.

5. The partners at the major consulting companies are very motivated individuals with very high compensation who must meet yearly consulting services sales quotas. In many ways, being a partner is a cushy job and the only people a partner really answers to is other partners. However, their yearly services sales quota hangs over them. In order to meet these sales quotas, they must place their consultants and this means selling or placing the consultants that have experience in the applications from the major software vendors (although consulting companies do occasionally place independent contractors on projects, they prefer not to as their margin on an independent consultant is much less than their margin on a full time employee).

6. Consulting companies are extremely hierarchical—I would say approaching that of a military organization. The resources below the partner level have no say in how the organization is managed. In fact, they don't even have a say on the technical recommendations that they make if they happen to contradict with the position that the partner wants to send to the client. If a recommendation is to be provided by a consultant, which may affect sales of consulting services, the recommendation will be run past the partner first. The partner will then tell the consultant what his or her "professional opinion" on the matter will be.

It should be relatively clear from the points listed above, but partners must be able to convince their clients to hire their consultants, who are trained in the applications from the major vendors. However, in order to convince their clients to staff their resources, they must also convince their clients to implement the software of the major vendors, as that is the expertise that their consultants offer. Thus, consulting companies have a conflict of interest when making recommendations regarding software selection.

To prove this, let's take a hypothetical example. Let's imagine a new partner joins IBM or Deloitte or any of the other major consulting companies (it does not matter which because they all operate in a similar fashion). Let's further imagine that this partner is truly focused on selecting the best software on the market to meet his or her client's requirements. An objective analysis would find that some of the best software available on the market to meet the client's needs is not the software for which the partner has trained resources. If the partner were "honest" and put the client's interests above his own, the partner would admit this fact to the client, increasing the likelihood that the client chooses a software vendor for which the partner has no resources that can be staffed. (At this point one might say that the partner could hire independent contractors to perform consulting, taking a lower margin on them. However, the contract market is well-developed for the major applications only, so for anything but the larger vendors, this is not an option.) As soon as the client chooses software, which the partner cannot staff, the partner loses out on both the services revenue and also their ability to control the implementation. If the client were to select an application from a smaller vendor, in most cases the consultants will come from that vendor as well. A partner that cannot staff as many resources on projects will eventually fail to meet their quota, and will be asked to leave the consulting company. Therefore, ***even if a partner wanted to (and having worked with many of them I can say that most of them don't care either way),*** they could not provide objective advice to their clients. This is the problem when any entity—not just consulting—receives a benefit if they advise a client to do one thing or another. This conflict of interest is rampant also in the financial industry, where recommendations are often made based upon the result that would maximize fees. Before moving on to the topic of how to interpret a consulting company's advice, I will finish off with a short story about how the large consulting companies operate.

I was at one time a manager at a large consulting company. During software training, I met a person who was in a management position at a company that was implementing the software I worked with. At the beginning of the training session we went around the room and stated the company for whom we worked. Once this person found out the company I worked for, he approached me and asked if I could pass on information to someone in my company about our support in selecting a consulting company for their implementation. I want to emphasize that this person was very clear that they wanted my company's help in selecting a consulting company, and not for actually performing the implementation.

I passed on this information to the partner to whom I reported. Because this was a fresh opportunity, I was besieged by phone calls from partners from around the country about how to handle the situation. One partner was of the opinion that the appropriate approach was to accept the consulting selection project under the false pretense that we would help them find the best consulting company for their needs, but in actual fact, we would impress them so much with what we had to offer that the client would simply call off the selection process and choose us instead. To carry out this partner's strategy, we would need to suppress information from the consulting companies that we were evaluating, but adjust the information so that it never seemed complete, and essentially stall the process so that the outcome would work to our advantage. It was not one rogue partner that recommended this approach, they all advised the same thing in one shape or form.

The selection phase of a project (be it software selection or implementation partner selection) is much shorter than the implementation stage and uses far fewer resources. Therefore, no consulting company that performs software selection and also has the capability and resources to perform the software implementation for a company will be satisfied with just the software selection work. In fact, a core strategy of every consulting company I have come into contact with is to use initial projects to gain larger projects. When I worked for KPMG I was told by a partner to snoop around for other work while I was there. Another partner used to repeat the phrase "penetrate and radiate" in meetings with large numbers of people and on conference calls (so it was not even a secret within the firm), so once into a client, you radiate through them by offering them more and more services. There is never even the pretense that services should be sold that the client actually needs—it is literally never even brought up in internal conversations. Consulting companies are generally unconcerned with whether these services are needed or appropriate, because at the end of the day it all comes down to billing hours, and the margin per hour.

Interpreting Information from Consulting Companies

One thing that I hope to establish is that all software selection information (and many other types of information) that comes from consulting companies is suspect. Depending on suspect information from consulting companies is one reason—and I will show many others—why quite often the software implemented by companies is inappropriate for their requirements. The software happened to be what the consultants that worked for the company were trained in and could bill for. Therefore, the software selected met the needs of the consulting company, but not the needs of the company making the actual software selection.

The misinformation provided by consulting companies for software selection goes beyond simply prompting their clients to choose software that is not the best for their needs. Consulting companies were instrumental in completely overselling the benefits of every major new software technology, with ERP being an excellent example of this. In the SCM Focus Press book, *The Real Story Behind ERP: Separating Fact from Fiction*, I cover the rather surprising result of my research that ERP has failed to live up to not just one, but also nearly all of the promises that were used to sell ERP systems to clients.

Consulting companies also misinform clients as to what they can expect in terms of the implementation effort, how well the software will work for them, and therefore their expected return on investment. When advising their clients, they follow a sales approach rather than a scientific approach. At times, the consulting companies I have worked for and worked with, as an independent consultant seem to be nothing more than sales arms for the largest software vendors (major consulting companies tend to have partnerships with only the largest software vendors). A good example of this was a webinar that I was asked to attend by one of my clients; a consulting company presented the webinar. I had worked with the application that was the topic of the webinar. However, throughout the webinar, this consulting company consistently presented a viewpoint about the application, one that I had never experienced even though I had worked on multiple projects with this software. According to this company, the application was "easy to install," "planners liked it," and "it just worked." Many of the statements they made were directly contradicted by my experience with this software on projects. However, when different companies that were logged into the webinar would ask a question, there was always a fast and easy answer for what could be done to mitigate the concern. The consultants who presented in the webinar were in full sales mode. They appeared to be willing to say anything in order to get the companies participating in the webinar interested in contacting them for consulting work. More detail on this experience is covered in an article that I wrote on this topic and is available at the link below:

http://www.scmfocus.com/productionplanningandscheduling/2012/11/16/ a-review-of-plan4demands-ppds-webinar/

Of course new implementations are all positive for consulting companies, as they provide the consulting services—they receive benefits with no risk. However, the implementing company takes a risk on every implementation. Therefore, the consulting company will have a strong tendency to be more Pollyannaish on the potential of the implementation than is warranted based upon experience. As an independent consultant I also interview to work as a consultant on implementation projects. From this experience I can say that there is simply no doubt that potential clients prefer to hear positive stories versus realistic stories regarding experiences with an application. So the consultants and consulting firms that offer the rosiest future scenarios have the highest potential to get the most work. This is of course not an isolated problem for software and consulting. Among lawyers it is well-known that those who paint a pretty picture to potential clients have a higher probability of getting more business.

Finding Entities That Lack Financial Bias

The only consulting companies that can be said to be without a financial conflict of interest are those that only perform the software selection and do not perform the implementation—if (and this is a big if) they are not resellers of the software. The same would be true of an independent consultant, although typically independent consultants are not hired to assist with software selection as this type of work tends to go to the large consulting companies that offer both software selection and implementation. However, while hiring an independent consultant or a consultant that only performs software selections addresses the financial bias, it does not control other types of bias. In my experience I have found many—if not most—of the consultants that work in my field have a strong bias toward the software that they work with. For example, at SCM Focus, I try to describe the reality of working with different software applications, and sometimes this means explaining the frustrating parts or poorly-designed parts of the application. There are several articles on the SCM Focus website about one particular application that had quite a few problems. I was actually contacted by a European independent consultant asking me not to do that, as it would decrease the demand for the application and by extension, his services. In other conversations, when I bring up some excellent functionality in a competing application and in my view, clearly superior functionality, the consultant will invariably say:

> *"Oh, well my application can do that. It may not do it the same way, but it does it."*

The fact that two entities can "do something," does not make them equal in doing that thing. I have observed that when the functionality is clearly inferior, the person defending the inferior product will use the term "different." I know of no other area of analysis where it would be accepted that because two items have something in common that they can be considered equal. For instance, both a bicycle and an airplane will get me from San Francisco to Los Angeles and the end result may be the same, but they are certainly not the same thing and they are not simply "different."

Therefore, if one is very careful, one can find entities in the market that do not have a financial bias. However, removing all bias is exceedingly difficult when contracting for consulting services. If someone who is advising you is to be taken seriously, at the very least they should not have a financial incentive based on your selection of a software application. Just achieving this modest goal would be a great improvement in the advice that you will receive over the current status quo.

Conclusion

Consulting companies are major influencers for enterprise software purchasing decisions. Consulting companies talk up their independence, but there is very little independence in decision-making or thought, particularly when a consulting company reaches any size. The evidence is that all of the major consulting companies make the same software recommendations. They recommend software that is from large vendors that they can staff themselves to bill the maximum number of hours.[14] This fact alone is a major reason why the enterprise software market is not competitive. The IT spend is misallocated in the system, and routed to less competitive offerings, and consulting companies are a major reason for this. Generally consulting companies also reduce the success ratio of enterprise software implementations. This is because so many applications that are selected are not the best fit for the client. In the vast majority of cases the application selected meets the business requirements to a much lower degree than other applications, which could have been purchased. Essentially contracting a large consulting company to provide selection advice is almost guaranteed to result in a bad software selection decision.

Large consulting companies are a bundle of conflicts of interest, and yet strangely, during the software selection process and while the consulting company is providing its "advice," this topic is not raised. The clients, as well as the consulting companies, all operate under the ludicrous assumption that the consulting company is actually looking after the client's interests. Large consulting companies want to limit all consultants from the software vendor because of both the desire to bill for the maximum number of consultants, and secondly, because having consultants from other entities on the project reduce their ability to control the account. This means having the project staffed almost exclusively by one's own consultants who are trained in just the applications from the largest vendors like SAP and Oracle. As soon as a smaller software vendor is selected, it means more non-consulting

---

[14] The lack of appreciation for this topic is quite shocking. If a person has 1,000 pounds of apples to sell, and no peaches, and they are asked which is better "apples or peaches," it's not hard to imagine which answer one will receive. Software buyers approach consulting companies that have just a few different types of fruit to sell, and thinking they will receive objective recommendations that will actually look at all of the fruit on the market.

employees are working with the client. I was once at a consulting meeting with a group of Deloitte managers and one of them was complaining that they could not reach their sales quota because the client had all these consultants working on the project that did not work for Deloitte and therefore they were not benefitting him personally. He had a strategy, which he shared with me, for getting these consultants from other companies off the project and replacing them with Deloitte consultants. One can imagine with these types of motivations continually working in the background how little any software recommendations from a consulting company has to do with what is the best choice for the client.

Both institutional analysis as well as my consulting experience support the fact that large consulting companies as well as most of the smaller consulting companies are making selection advice based upon their own revenue goals and that their client's interests do not factor into the advice they provide. The major consulting companies have hundreds of thousands of consultants working for them. A large percentage of them work in software implementation, with the more senior members working at least part time in software selection. However, not a single one of them can admit what is entirely obvious, that the software selection recommendations offered by their company has nothing to do with what is right for the client. Any consultant who did admit this either with a client or in any public forum would be quickly reprimanded and would either hurt their career, or they would simply be fired.

I have sometimes given advice to smaller software vendors, and on occasion the topic of working with a large consulting company to have their software recommended has come up. I have repeatedly told these software vendors not to waste their time courting large consulting companies. I gave this advice to one software vendor years ago, and they still scheduled a meeting with a partner from Ernst and Young. I attended this meeting. The message delivered from the Ernst and Young partner was that if this small software vendor brought a client to him, he would be willing to staff that project with his consultants. The small software vendor would have to train the Ernst and Young consultants in the application, and then they would bill the client at top dollar for a project Ernst and Young had not originated. That is the type of arrangement that small and even medium sized software vendors can expect from big consulting companies.

CHAPTER 7

How to Use the Reports of Analyst Firms Like Gartner

In many cases Gartner's analysis cannot be used properly without adjusting the research output. By most analysts' accounts, only about 20 percent of the research that Gartner performs actually gets into a report. While Gartner publishes reports, it prefers to deliver more information by having clients consult with analysts. The downside to this, of course, is that consulting is more expensive.

Much of this book was dedicated to providing the background necessary for the reader to understand why Gartner reports must be adjusted. Companies can, of course, contact Gartner and ask questions, but at a cost. There are some things that can be adjusted without contacting Gartner, and some things that cannot. I have included some of the most common adjustments, and have listed those items that would require a company to contact Gartner to get more information.

Gartner Report Adjustment Rules

Never Use Just the Gartner Magic Quadrant to Make a Purchasing Decision

This point should be self-evident, especially if you have read the rest of the book up to this point. According to Louis Columbus, *"IT buyers regrettably sometimes make their entire purchasing decision just on the Quadrant alone."* It is hard to know where to begin as there are so many reasons not to do this, but as I have explained, Gartner's methodology for their Magic Quadrant includes factors that have nothing to do with the benefit to enterprise software buyers. Instead, the criteria are metrics that could be used by investors contemplating buying the software vendor's stock. Secondly, even Gartner does not want buyers or investors making decisions based simply upon the Magic Quadrant or any other research they produce. One should consider the research produced by Gartner as a "starter kit" to start the ball rolling for more analysis, contracting with Gartner for more analyst services, etc.

Adjust the Rankings for the Vendor's Size

Gartner prefers large software vendors. This large vendor orientation is clear, and it is difficult to see how a person doing a complete analysis on this topic could find that this bias does not exist.

On the web there are several statements by Gartner analysts that Gartner does *not* favor large vendors. Other than managing perception, I can't think of a single good reason for anyone to say this. To believe that Gartner does not favor large vendors, one would have to both not understand the various Gartner methodologies and not read the Gartner research output.

A vendor's size is not a universal positive. Bigger vendors are less responsive, particularly if the buyer is not a large client. Because bigger vendors offer a broader set of products, they are constantly trying to capture more and more footprint within their existing clients, and they are not going to be happy selling a single application to a client. Larger vendors are less focused on their products, less focused on R&D, and more focused on marketing and on their partnerships with major consulting companies.

One of the reasons I enjoy keeping up with smaller best-of-breed vendors is because they have less bureaucracy, and they engage in far more innovation than the big vendors. I implement the software of the large vendors, and when I visit smaller vendors, I always feel as if I have traveled forward in time because the approaches we follow in SAP are so dated. I essentially implement approaches and technologies that are little changed from the mid-1990s. And of course, bigger vendors are more expensive (see the section on Adjusting for Price on page 92).

So, the bigger vendors in any Magic Quadrant are simply overrated by Gartner. The best way to account for this is by reducing their rating, although I cannot provide a specific percentage of adjustment.

Insert More Reality into Gartner's Ratings

Generally speaking, Gartner analysts do not have hands-on experience with the applications they are rating. Most of the Gartner analysts have at least fifteen years of experience in their area, so it is not that they lack experience but they usually lack implementation experience. Gartner analysts do speak with people in companies that implement software, but they speak at the level of CIOs and vice presidents. This constant interaction with senior executives at companies that buy enterprise software is a main reason why working for Gartner is considered to be such a good place to create contacts for future careers. However, these high-level people do not use the applications that they purchase; they pass along information to Gartner analysts that is already second-hand! While executives at buyers certainly know the problems that they face on implementations, overseeing implementations and actually working with the software are two different things.

Steps to Increase Reality of the Software Selection

Now that we have established that Gartner's ratings require more reality, the question is "how." An effective software selection will combine the high-level analysis provided by Gartner (provided either by reading research or by interacting with Gartner analysts) with more detailed analysis of:

- How the application actually works

- How the employees of the company will actually use the application

- How it will be configured and fit in with the rest of the company's footprint

Unfortunately, this is a lot more work and cannot be done by those who are the decision makers for the software selection. So, this more detailed work tends not to get done. However, it should be done—if not for all the applications under consideration then at the very least for the applications that the company finds the most intriguing. This applies to both buyers and investors, and is accomplished by having technical resources participate in the software selection process. I have no idea why so many executives think they are qualified to analyze statements made by presales consultants, but usually presentations are made to buyers with no one in the meeting from the buyer's side who can validate the technical statements made by the vendor's representatives.

Finding Technical Fact Checkers

Many times individuals with technical backgrounds can be pulled from the buyer's IT department. However, this is not always the case, especially if there is no one familiar with the category of application being analyzed. I include a section on hiring independent consultants who can provide expertise that may not be available inside your company.

Viewing demos that are performed by a vendor's most skilled presales consultants is not a good way to truly understand an application. Rather than scripted demos, a more reality-based approach is to allow the reviewers to ask more questions and drive more of the demo. I cover this topic in more detail in the book *Enterprise Software Selection*.

Adjust Down the Rate of Predicted Change

Gartner tends to overestimate the amount of change that occurs in any one software category, as well as the business developments in that category. Also, Gartner will describe industry trends as being more legitimate and permanent than they actually are. For instance, in my area, many companies have initiatives to move toward a make-to-order environment; however, because of the limitations of the approach, most never will. This falls under the category of a "pipe dream."

It's easy to get the impression that because Gartner learns about these initiatives from senior executives within the buying companies, Gartner tends to take their word for it that most of these initiatives will succeed, when in fact a higher percentage may fail. This dynamic applies equally on both the buyer and the vendor side, as Gartner will frequently get on-board with a new technology initiative before a vendor and before that initiative has had the time to prove itself. For instance, in my field Gartner has been a major proponent of something called SAP Hana.[15] However, while the volume of the talk about Hana has been turned up for several years, I have yet to see its effect on any of my projects. I do not want to digress, as this is a separate and technical topic, but SAP Hana is really just something SAP should be doing anyway without a massive marketing offensive. It is simply a way to leverage evolving hardware and database technologies, and is really no big deal. In fact, I am surprised SAP and other vendors had not provided these options years earlier, as I began leveraging them myself on my own hardware several years ago. As I have stated previously, very little innovation happens at large software vendors. Small vendors put in the R&D and take the risk, and the large vendors copy the technology and crank up the marketing volume. When you control your customer base and have relationships with large consulting companies that recommend your product, no matter its utility, to their clients, innovation is simply not necessary. This is discussed in detail in the following link:

http://www.scmfocus.com/enterprisesoftwarepolicy/2012/03/11/why-the-largest-enterprise-software-companies-have-no-reason-to-innovate/

I have witnessed several innovations that no IT analyst firm has written anything about (one of which I covered in the book *Supply Chain Forecasting Software*). After a large firm has copied the technology, I assume I will read about how great it is in a Gartner report, maybe five years from now. In any case Gartner jumped on the Hana bandwagon while it was simply an experimental product. If Hana were released from a smaller vendor, it is highly unlikely that it would have been promoted by Gartner.

---

[15] The technology behind Hana is a huge yawn. It amounts to using solid state devices and new database structures that can handle very large data sets, and leverages SAP's database acquisitions to lock out Oracle from its accounts. In terms of the technology, these are things SAP should be doing anyway. A few years ago I ordered a laptop with a solid state drive because computers run better on them. I have also assembled multiple solid state drives in benchmarking tests of a planning system. However, I did not take out a press release after I did this. There are other areas of Hana that are adjustments to the database design and allow for faster table access. These are primarily for improving reporting speed.

As I hope the previous example demonstrates, Gartner is well-known for its Hype Cycle analysis, but Gartner itself will help drive a Hype Cycle to the "Peak of Inflated Expectations" (using Gartner's own Hype Cycle terminology). Often they are more swayed by how much "sense" a vendor's explanation seems to be over how it actually works in practice. Unfortunately, a lot of things seem like a good idea or seem to make sense but don't necessarily take flight. For example, SaaS was supposed to be the next great thing, but its adoption has been slow. Hypothetically, Gartner's frequent interaction with buyers should enable them to keep from doing this. However, my research into their past reports indicate that this is a consistent theme of Gartner despite their access to buyers that would allow them to validate vendors' statements.

Therefore, Gartner's reports should be adjusted and deferred. Whatever Gartner is predicting, it almost certainly will not happen as quickly as predicted. It should be understood that while many buyers may be moving in a particular direction, many will not be successful. Many initiatives are simply trends, and when they peter out, they are renamed. In my area, there is an initiative referred to as "lean," a rebranding of many identical initiatives of JIT (just in time), which mostly flamed out back in the 1980s. Lean is already running its course, and after it is not longer sellable, the consultants will come up with a new name for the same philosophies. There are now roughly half a million books on "lean," but the actual impact on inventory management?[16] Negligible. The benefit to consulting revenues of consultancies promoting lean concepts? Priceless.

Likewise, vendors frequently bring out new ideas and products, but most of these developments tend to be transitory and some are really just rebranding of old concepts by sales and marketing. Secondly, beyond time-phasing Gartner's predictions, many of their projections will never come to pass. When reviewing Gartner's past predictions, I found this repeatedly. Gartner's Hype Cycle proposes a consistent and eventual movement of technologies to the "Plateau of Productivity." However, some technologies or ideas are never implemented broadly and many disappear all together.

---

[16] Yes, I am joking. However, it is one of the most popular topics for publication in the supply chain management and production management space.

When No Magic Quadrant Exists

One of the biggest obstacles that a buyer or analyst can face is when there is no Magic Quadrant for the software category of interest. When Gartner decides to create a Magic Quadrant for a group of products or a software suite, it is impossible for a company, which only makes a single product, to compete in that type of analysis. Secondly, it is generally inadvisable for a buyer to implement multiple products from one suite. Doing this means using a vendor's weak products along with its stronger products, and in fact is the primary way that bad products are able to get sold. Without a connection to an ERP system, or as part of a suite, it is much more difficult for a bad product to get purchased. Also, once the analysis moves to the suite level, the business tends to get the short end of the stick, because at that point it simply becomes more about integration, and the functionality becomes an afterthought.

Nevertheless, software suites has been a common approach to IT implementation for several decades. While the concept was that there would be fewer integration issues if software suites were implemented, this approach has not meant the reduction in integration costs that were promised by ERP systems. This is explained in my book *The Real Story Behind ERP: Separating Fact from Fiction*.

Furthermore, this has meant that the business does not get the software it needs. Software selection based on software suites does not emphasize each application, but instead emphasizes the suite. As explained in this quote from Christopher Koch of *CIO Magazine*, software suites themselves are mechanisms that reduce the competition a vendor must face.

> *"Indeed, integration standards interfere with ERP vendors' traditional ways of gaining and keeping customers and market share. Before the Web came along, your integration strategy was simple: Buy as many pre integrated applications from a single vendor as possible. That worked for you, and it worked extremely well for the vendor; integrated application suites fetched a high price and required long-term maintenance and support contracts that promised a steady, predictable stream of revenue from customers."*—ABCs of ERP

I have now seen many poor-performing applications implemented and a great deal of frustration on the part of business users and managers who were not delivered applications that ever had a chance of meeting their requirements. Such high-level Magic Quadrants are not useful to a company that is selecting an application that is a subcategory of that Magic Quadrant.

If a company is looking to select one or multiple products from a suite, it's difficult to see how a high-level Magic Quadrant of this type can be adjusted. Some detail about specific applications can be provided in the vendor description section, but this is simply not enough detail to support an informed decision. At this point, the Gartner analyst must be contacted, and there is little value that can be received from the Magic Quadrant by itself.

Adjusting for Functionality and Maintainability

Gartner employs analysts with a strong tendency to look at the bigger (biggest?) possible picture. Gartner looks at so many factors outside of how good the application actually is and how maintainable the solution is, that these most important factors are under-emphasized. Corporate buyers should strive to obtain the software that closely matches their business requirements and has the very best functionality. Gartner essentially tells buyers that the application is really just one component to the decision, but the problem is that Gartner has too many factors pulling their ratings away from practical software implementation criteria. This can be addressed by checking reference accounts and by asking the Gartner analyst how the various vendors performed on the surveys for functionality and maintainability.

Disregarding Gartner's Deeper Technology Insights and Predictions

In their reports, Gartner will sometimes make technology projections or try to describe the technology. I have found quite a few of these statements to be unreliable. Gartner shows no evidence of being predictive; there is no reason to pay attention to their predictions.[17] Furthermore, Gartner's technology prediction opinions have been lampooned in numerous articles on the Internet, by authors

---

[17] Gartner acquired a prominent IT analyst firm that specialized in my software category: AMR Research. Not only was AMR Research sometimes wrong, AMR was spectacularly wrong as I explain in this article: http://www.scmfocus.com/scmhistory/2010/07/how-analysts-got-everything-wrong-on-marketplaces/

who are experts in that particular category of technology. A number of the technology predictions I have read seem to have been designed to create a splash, rather than to stand the test of time. One that definitely sticks out as ludicrous was the prediction by Gartner that the Windows Phone would become the second most popular smartphone platform between 2012 and 2015 and account for 19.5% market share. 2015 is not yet upon us, but the Windows Phone has only 3.2% market share. Another example is taken from their prediction on SaaS, which is a quotation I also used in Chapter 2.

> *"'Up until now, the unique nature of the software market has meant that buyers had very little negotiating power after the initial purchase of a software license,' Gartner Vice President William Snyder said in a research note. 'We expect those dynamics to change considerably over the next 5 to 10 years, giving CIOs and software procurement officers more bargaining power while potentially reducing software vendor profit margins.*
>
> *"Gartner also predicts that a fourth of all new business software will be delivered by software as a service by 2011.'"*

Software costs have not significantly declined as predicted by Gartner. Gartner also overshot their second prediction that a fourth of all software would be delivered as SaaS by 2011. As of 2012, software delivered by SaaS represents only four percent of total software sales. Granted, SaaS software is less expensive than on-premises software, so the number of seats served is no doubt higher than its sales percentage. But it's difficult to see how the delivery of SaaS as a percentage of all enterprise software would be anywhere close to the twenty-five percent value of software delivery estimated by Gartner.

Was this bad analysis on the part of Gartner? Based upon the enormous advantages that SaaS has in terms of cost and time to deploy, as well as the efficiency of central administration by the vendor, I believe Gartner's projections were reasonable at the time. However, what many people who predicted a faster growth failed to consider were issues ranging from security concerns to the lower customizability of SaaS solutions, as well as the perception of integration issues that prevented SaaS from taking off as initially expected. The fact of the matter is that technology prediction is a difficult business. However, Gartner is not correct enough of the time for it to be taken seriously. Gartner has not demonstrated any special aptitude for technology prediction. On the other hand, if your client base does not notice Gartner's prediction track record, and if the bold predictions make for good marketing copy, then I suppose there is no reason to stop.

For those looking for technology predictions, Forrester has a better reputation for being right than Gartner.

Adjusting for Price

Gartner does not account for price in their rankings. Instead they compare all products as if they are in the same cost category. This approach creates a bias toward more expensive products. In addition, because Gartner's methodology ranks larger vendors higher, Gartner's recommendations tend to push buyers to higher-priced products and products that result in higher consulting costs. (Larger vendors tend to have both higher acquisition costs and higher consulting costs.) Therefore, it makes the most sense to adjust Gartner's ratings for price. Unfortunately, this is not an easy task.

There are few software vendors like Arena Solutions and Demand Works that post the cost of their software on their websites. In fact, in many years working in the field of software implementation, I am rarely informed of the actual costs of the software being installed. Many vendors are cagey about their price; among a host of factors, the price depends upon the number of seats and how much the software vendor wants the account. Determining the actual costs is time consuming and requires a significant amount of interaction with the software vendor so they can "understand their requirements."

Gartner is perfectly positioned to provide some type of rough approximation of the cost of the software, which could allow buyers to put some vendors out of their cost range. They are also well-positioned to estimate the consulting/implementation and maintenance costs of the different vendors per software category. However, if a company does not want to use a Gartner analyst to answer these questions, the company can adjust for Gartner's large vendor bias (and by extension their bias toward expensive solutions bias). They can push a smaller vendor up in consideration in order to account for lower cost and better value, if of course the vendor has other compelling factors. This leads to the next area of adjustment.

Adjusting for the Buying Company's Size

Gartner's bias toward larger vendors is related partially to Gartner's belief that companies prefer (or should prefer) to buy from the largest vendors. However, while larger buyers may prefer to purchase from larger vendors, it is less true of smaller buyers. Of course, Gartner's largest customers are the biggest companies in the world.

I do not know if smaller buyers would prefer buying from larger buyers if they could afford to do so, but the fact is that smaller buyers often can't. Generally, small innovative vendors offer point solutions, have small deal sizes, and sell to small buyers. As the vendor grows, it is able to increase the size of buyers to which it sells. Therefore, Gartner's ratings fit the preferences (and checkbook) of large buyers far more than they do for smaller companies. Experience over time will let the smaller buyer know who they can afford to buy from, so for smaller buyers it is a simple matter to remove all or the majority of the largest vendors from their list and to focus on the other vendors.

Conclusion

While Gartner publishes reports, companies that buy subscriptions receive only a small percentage of their research. In order to maximize their revenues they prefer to deliver more information by having clients consult with analysts. The downside to this of course is that consulting is more expensive. This chapter was designed to prepare buyers to work in a more cost effective manner with Gartner. One should consider the research produced by Gartner as a "starter kit" to start the ball rolling for more analysis, contracting with Gartner for more analyst services, etc. Gartner's research can be adjusted by adjusting downward the rankings for the larger vendors, as they are inflated. Secondly, as an implementer myself, Gartner's research often makes me uncomfortable because it is at such a high level. In the software categories that are my areas of expertise the analyst writing the report clearly does not have enough hands-on experience to explain the reality of the implementation issues that will be faced during the implementation, and a consultation with the analyst is not going to change their knowledge level. Gartner does a nice job of using surveys to uncover implementation challenges faced by clients with different software, but even still, this does not adequately find its way back into the Magic Quadrant ratings as my example of the highly problematic SAP BW product should demonstrate. This chapter explained how to add more reality into the software selection process, and I consider this to be one of the most important parts of software selection. Adjusting down the predicted rate of change is necessary because Gartner tends to overestimate this in their analysis. Initiatives are frequently announced with great fanfare, but most of them fail to find any purchase within organizations. Executives both overestimate the degree of innovation occurring within their own companies, and are naturally persuasive individuals, which is a major reason they have the positions that they do. Gartner often appears to be drinking the Kool-Aid that is served by the buyers they interview. However, there is an optimism bias as the executives will always be confident of new initiatives within the company. Gartner's Kool-Aid drinking extends to vendors as well, particularly large vendors.

Another area that must be adjusted is functionality and maintainability. Gartner underestimates the importance of both of these dimensions of software implementation. The functionality is critical to the ROI and probability of success of the implementation. Because Gartner underemphasizes functionality, it has the consequence of promoting the purchase of riskier applications. In terms of maintainability, Gartner had clear evidence of the maintenance problems with SAP BW, yet they continued to list SAP in the Leader Quadrant. Certainly, the fact that SAP is the largest business intelligence software vendor makes them a "leader" in terms of their market share—and this is of course quite important to investors. However, it's unclear how simply having a large market share helps an application be maintained by a buyer. If the lowest quality offering, an application with very significant implementation and maintainability issues can be listed in the Leader Quadrant, then Gartner's Magic Quadrant must be adjusted by buyers because these dimensions are of more importance to the buyer than they are being weighted by Gartner. The price of applications must be adjusted for by buyers. Gartner does not rate either the actual application cost, nor the TCO in the Magic Quadrant, so the most expensive solutions are placed on equal footing with the least expensive. However, the price is important to buyers and therefore, looking at a Magic Quadrant without adding price into the equation would not make much sense.

CHAPTER 8

How to Interpret Vendor-Provided Information to Reduce Project Risk

Software sales is known as one of the more aggressive types of sales. Good software salesmen are highly compensated, and are given every incentive to sell as much as possible. In some cases, such as a software company for whom I worked called i2 Technologies, the salespeople were so out of control in their lust to sell that they actually derailed the company. This orientation began at the very top of the company. The head of sales for i2 Technologies was famously to have remarked in a highly-charged sales meeting (all i2 sales gatherings tended to be highly-charged affairs):

> *"I never want to hear the excuse that software does not exist as reason to not sell."*

Information about software comes from either sales or marketing. Marketing includes the development of collateral materials, both printed materials and the website copy, which are designed to put the company's products in the best possible light. Both sales and marketing are under a great deal of pressure to compete with statements and literature provided by other companies. A big part of sales and marketing is about creating a vision, which has nothing to do with communicating real features in software.

Marketing Literature

Software vendor marketing literature can take the form of pamphlets or website copy, and can be quite easy to get hold of. This literature is very influential in software selection but, depending upon the vendor, often contains false information and is unreliable. For example, I have read numerous marketing documents that explain how a product performed "inventory optimization" (a particular set of mathematics for supply planning), when the software discussed did not actually possess this functionality. The videos below explain more.

http://vimeo.com/14844814

http://blip.tv/scm-focus/google-search-for-misuse-of-inventory-optimization-4122062

To provide further examples and explain what I mean, I have extracted quotes from some marketing literature. Below are some lines from SAP's marketing literature on their product NetWeaver, called SAP NetWeaver, interspersed with my critique on their statements. My critiques appear so frequently because the falsehoods are so prevalent throughout the document.

> *"The SAP NetWeaver technology platform is a comprehensive integration and application platform that helps reduce your total cost of ownership (TCO)."*

NetWeaver is not actually a product but a marketing construct; it is simply nomenclature added on to existing, mostly IT infrastructure, products thus making this statement untrue. As is covered at our companion site, Software Decisions, SAP has the highest total cost of ownership in any software category in which it offers a product.[18]

---

[18] The Software Decisions website is available at http://www.softwaredecisions.org

"It facilitates the integration and alignment of people, information, and business processes across organizational and technological boundaries."

No, it does not. NetWeaver only relates to infrastructure, and does not help out a client in areas outside of infrastructure, and not to belabor the point, but NetWeaver is itself not a distinct product.

"SAP NetWeaver easily integrates information and applications from virtually any source."

No, it does not. None of the products that were placed within the "NetWeaver umbrella," which relate to integration, the most prominent being SAP PI,[19] enables integration any easier than other integration products. In fact, SAP PI is not even competitive with other applications in the same category. Companies primarily buy SAP PI because they either can't differentiate good integration software from bad integration software, or they think that they will be able to leverage SAP-to-SAP integration capabilities. Those individuals familiar with both applications would not support the idea that SAP PI is competitive with enterprise integration products such as Informatica. In fact, SAP misrepresents application integration completely with this sentence. Integration is always work—files must be transformed and converted to match with the data requirements of the receiving system. Jobs must be setup to carry the data from one application to another, and it must be scheduled in a way to run automatically. No application has been developed that makes integration "easy" anymore than a battery has been developed to easily store power. In fact, SAP PI makes application integration more difficult than other vendors. This should not be surprising, because ERP vendors have no special knowledge or ability to develop superior applications in this area. Application integration, like power storage, is always complex, and both have proven immune to magical promises about how transformative they would be. Vendors, not just SAP, have been pitching easy integration for decades now, and integration still is problematic, and still consumes a consistent percentage of the IT budget of buying companies.

---

[19] SAP PI stands for "process integration," but it is really just an integration application. It was misnamed for marketing reasons.

> *"It interoperates with and can be extended using the primary market technologies—Microsoft .NET, Sun's J2EE, and IBM WebSphere. SAP NetWeaver is the technical foundation for mySAP™ Business Suite and SAP® xApps™ and ensures maximum reliability, security, and scalability, so your mission-critical business processes run smoothly."*

This is the technical gobblygook portion of the document. The intent here is to throw so many terms at the reader (who is typically an executive and is not familiar with these technologies) so that they will be impressed. It is also very unspecific about how this would all work, so the reader has to take the author's word for it. Many of the terms that are used in this quotation are already no longer relevant. I have already addressed the fact that NetWeaver is a meaningless term. The term "mySAP Business Suite" is no longer used, but it never was anything beyond a collection of other SAP products. The xApp program was a "brand" that held out the potential to smaller vendors of getting into SAP projects. In fact, the xApp program was a giant competitive intelligence operation, which allowed SAP to take intellectual property from other vendors in order to bring out competing products. I called for the xApp program to be discontinued or investigated by the Federal Trade Commission shortly after it came out, as the article below describes.

http://www.scmfocus.com/inventoryoptimizationmultiechelon/2010/01/its-time-for-the-sap-xapps-program-to-die/

However, the xApp program is now, in fact, dead.

> *"This Web services-based platform offers a comprehensive, tightly integrated set of capabilities. And by providing preconfigured business content, SAP helps reduce the need for custom integration and lowers your TCO."*

I work on SAP projects for a living, and this document is a few years old now, but I have never seen any of these "products" used on a project. I never saw any "preconfigured business content" and have never heard of this term used by anyone on any project at any time. SAP still has some of the highest integration costs of any application vendor because of the nature of their data backend, which does not allow the underlying relational database to be directly addressed. As I stated several paragraphs ago, SAP has always had the highest TCO (total cost of ownership) of any application I have reviewed, and continues to have the highest TCO.

> *"Enterprise Services Architecture is also a blueprint for complete business integration. Regardless of the functional or technical barriers and isolated applications that may have grown up over time in your company, Enterprise Services Architecture brings back flexibility, allowing you to design complete solutions that span all people who participate in your value chain, all information that is relevant to you, and all systems that are involved for each business process or problem. This means that you can now respond to workers' needs for business processes that are driven by collaborative, knowledge-based, and team-based processes rather than by isolated applications."*

No, it isn't. Not only do the products that pre-existed "NetWeaver" and were then added under the NetWeaver umbrella, not have the magical properties described in this quotation, they are not even competitive products. Workers in companies where SAP has been implemented do not have more responsive systems than other environments; they have decidedly less responsive systems. The last part of the quotation is pure hyperbole.

In one part of the document, SAP breaks down the benefits of NetWeaver by the different areas:

> *"Portal infrastructure—Gives workers unified, personalized, and role-based access to heterogeneous IT environments. Increases the efficiency of business processes spanning customers, suppliers, partners, and employees."*

SAP has been trying to get its portals used for more than a decade now, and they are still not used. SAP has a portal, but the potential that companies will benefit from it is low if they don't use it. Now I almost never hear about portals on projects.

> *"Knowledge management—Manages and makes accessible*
> *unstructured information such as text files, slide shows, or audio*
> *files. Includes integrated search, content management, publishing,*
> *classification, and workflow capabilities, as well as an open*
> *framework for third-party repositories."*

SAP has a product called Solution Manager, which has a few advantages in terms of documenting the implementation and allows Solution Manager to take you directly to configuration within the application. I analyze Solution Manager in the article below:

http://www.scmfocus.com/sapprojectmanagement/2012/01/the-end-of-sap-solution-manager/

However, these other things described in this quote either do not exist or are so overstated that they do not communicate what SAP's knowledge management products use. Furthermore, Solution Manager is really only used (and lightly used at that) by configurators like me. Solution Manager is not used in the way described above and no other portal, which SAP may offer to clients, works in that way.

> *"Business intelligence—Enables organizations to integrate, analyze,*
> *and disseminate business-critical information. Includes a robust*
> *suite of tools for creating and publishing customized, interactive*
> *reports and applications, which supports your decision making at*
> *every level."*

Business intelligence, which is covered by SAP's BI and Business Objects products, is not any more robust than any other reporting platform. In fact, according to the research firm Gartner, SAP has the lowest scores for both software quality and customer support of any application vendor in the space. I rarely see SAP BW add value for clients; in fact in most cases BI reports are missing in action.

> *"Master data management—Promotes information integrity across*
> *the business network in heterogeneous IT environments. Provides*

*services to consolidate, harmonize, and centrally manage your master
data, including business partner information, product master and
structures, and technical-asset information."*

SAP brought out a master data management product called MDM. However, it
never gained much of a following and had many implementation problems. It was
not competitive with other master data solutions in the marketplace.

I could go on and on about SAP's marketing documentation, but hopefully you get
the point. And while SAP takes enormous liberties with the truth, most vendor
marketing documentation is in some way misleading. In fact, aside from entertain-
ment value, there is little reason to read SAP's marketing literature. However, this
is not always the case with all vendors. For instance, a vendor whose marketing
documentation is quite accurate is Arena Solutions, a vendor that makes bill of
material management software and for which I wrote a book that featured their
software. I have never read any documentation from Arena that seems "off" or mis-
representative, and in fact a very good amount of Arena's documentation is quite
educational. This is, in fact, what marketing documentation should be, but is very
rarely the case because most companies cannot resist embellishing in order to make
their case and to persuade in the hopes of selling more software. Let's review some
of Arena's statements from their marketing literature to see how it differs from SAP.

*"Item management is easy when part data, assemblies and
documents—including drawings and data sheets—are all in one place.
Give your team and designated suppliers controlled access to all the
information they need to design and manufacture your product.*

*A centralized product record allows your team to make faster and
more efficient design decisions—like **reusing part specifications**
from old designs—and save time and money."*

This is all true. When all information is in one place it's easier to find, and in fact
Arena's software does just this. Arena's product also significantly increases the
reuse of old designs. Observe that the hyperbole of these statements is minimal,
and when contrasted to the highly-generalized statements that SAP made in their

marketing literature for NetWeaver, these statements are quite specific. Arena is not saying their software will do everything, but that it will do something specific, and then explains how it will do that thing.

> *"Create a unique record for every part in your item master with customizable part numbering schemes and categories. Customizable categories can be used to determine the layout and sequence of fields in your part record. With up to **250 customizable attributes** per category, BOMControl allows you to record and track the data you need, at big-picture and granular levels."*

Again, more specifics are provided by Arena of what they can do. Arena's application can hold up to 250 customizable attributes per category. A person who works in this area should have no problem understanding exactly what this means.

> *"Immediately see what's changed in any version of your bill of materials with a simple toggle to Redline mode.*
>
> *"Stop wasting time with phone calls or notes explaining every small change you've made to your BOM. When you grant supplier access to your contract manufacturers, they can see for themselves exactly what you've modified and how it impacts the overall product.*
>
> *"Quickly compare multiple BOMs to see what has changed, or what is different. Optimize procurement and production with side-by-side bill of materials comparisons that reveal component needs across multiple product lines."*

These statements tell the reader quite a bit. They explain how a company can stop wasting time by leveraging Arena's functionality with regard to managing revisions. The BOM can be compared to see what has changed and procurement and production can be managed by component need across multiple product lines.

This is just a sampling of Arena's marketing literature of course, but all of Arena's literature reads this way. One can learn a lot from reading Arena's literature because they describe a reality, not only of their software, but also of the environment in which their software is implemented. On the other hand, it is very difficult to learn by reading SAP's marketing literature (and the marketing literature of many other vendors) because they are so busy selling, that they have no time or space to educate. SAP's explanations are absolutely overwhelming, as if they are attempting to include as many accolades as they can. They attempt to sell the reader *in every possibly sentence* instead of selling the reader on the overall paper. In fact, SAP's marketing literature is insulting to one's intelligence and to one's time. SAP marketing literature is not so much read as it is "parsed."

How to Read and Differentiate Vendor Marketing Literature
In addition to learning from vendor marketing literature, there are more benefits. For example, more often than not, vendors who engage in extreme exaggerations and hyperbole are problematic vendors who are selling "pie in the sky." The marketing literature is telling you something about the company. The company who is ready and willing to sell you a bunch of baloney and has no standards for truth in their documentation will have a strong tendency to behave that way in other parts of the company and in their dealings with you. By reading between the lines of their literature, you can learn to steer clear of these vendors.

In addition, misleading marketing literature impacts the sales and presales groups of software vendors. Individuals who work in sales and presales rarely get first-hand experience with the application. Much of what they know about products comes from the marketing literature. They don't spend the time to talk with consultants who implement the software to determine what is true and what is not, and learn to be as accurate as possible. Most individuals simply don't care. If the marketing literature says that the vendor has developed a time machine, the sales group is going to go out and sell time machines. And of course as a buyer, it's your job to steer clear of companies selling time machines.

The Demo
The software demonstration (or demo) is one of the few opportunities to get first-hand experience with the software. Most information on demos (and there is not a lot to be found) explains how to put on a good demo. However, I could find nothing on how to get good value from a demo if you are the software buyer. There are

several issues that negatively affect how accurately demos can be said to represent reality. However, from the perspective of buyers, the weaknesses of demos are that they tend to be artificial and are controlled by the vendor.

The common issues with demos are listed below:

1. The company's presales consultant typically runs demos. The demo is not an accurate representation of how the software will actually be used because this person specializes in knowing all the ins and outs of the software and is typically quite specialized in that application. Users will never attain the ease-of-use demonstrated by the consultant because they use several applications throughout the day and won't gain the same depth of knowledge about the product as the consultant. Therefore, the consultant's level of knowledge allows them to make the product look much easier to use than it really is, and to gloss over its imperfections.

2. Demos use dummy data, which provides a great deal of flexibility to the presales consultant who drives the demo. Applications run faster and more smoothly with smaller data sets.

3. Demos tend to be tightly controlled in that they follow a script. The script makes the application look much more fluid and fully featured than it actually will be when implemented.

4. Too often the users are excluded from the demo, meaning that the demo tends to be a high-level affair. However, it is the users who ask the most pertinent questions related to how the software would be used in an everyday setting.

5. The same bullet point above applies for technology resources. They are needed to ask questions related to how the software actually works under the covers, how it loads and updates data, makes decisions, etc.

6. Demos tend to be short. Most range from between forty-five minutes to an hour. This is not enough time to explore an application, particularly if it is complex. Large audiences tend to shorten demos because the demo is often seen as just one part of the presentation that day, and the more senior members tend to want to spend an hour on several occasions going

over software. This short exposure time to the actual software is a mistake because the shorter the demo, generally the more the vendor can hide.

7. While I have never heard this mentioned in other published material on software selection, I find it very useful to have screenshots sent of interesting functionality. Once a buyer has screen shots they can mark up the screenshots, and then compare and contrast to screen shots of other applications. Comparing and contrasting functionality in this way is something I do when I choose software to showcase in books. This can allow a software selection document to be created that really explains the specific differences between the different vendors.

All this being said, demos are extremely important. While it should be remembered that the vendor would like to control the demo, ultimately, the *buyer* is in control of how the demo progresses—*if the buyer wants to take that control.* It is the buyer's time that is being taken and the purpose of the demo is to inform the buyer if this is the right application for them.

The best way to take control of a demo is to declare how you would like the demo to run, and to do so well in advance of the vendor actually making the presentation. Without this communication prior to the presentation, the software presales consultant can legitimately say that she is not prepared to perform the demo in that manner. This is because demos must be prepared both in terms of the data that is used and how the presales consultant manages the demo. Most presales consultants are not comfortable with individuals from the buyer navigating through the application himself or herself, so they must be told beforehand if these individuals would like to do so. However, this can be accomplished even if the demo is not performed in person because all screen-sharing applications allow transfer control of the computer to anyone who is part of the screen sharing session. Another way of taking control of the demo is to stop the flow of the presales consultant's presentation. The presales consultant may have a set of things he wants to show, and plan on leaving questions until later, but this is a way of taking control of the demo. As a buyer, you should remember that the entire purpose of the demo is for you to understand whether this software should be selected. Therefore, the presales consultant's desires must rank as a distant second to the buyer's needs.

Ways to make demos more useful to the buyer can be determined by working backward from the limitations of demos:

1. The presales consultant can explain the software, but someone else should drive the demo, at least for part of it. By doing so, you are controlling the presales consultant's skill level. Yes, certainly a presales consultant can move very quickly between the screens, but how intuitive is the application for a first-time user? If I take the example of SAP versus Arena Solutions, SAP allows companies that have included SAP in their software selection process to view their software only through the presentation of a software consultant. Arena Solutions allows anyone to self-navigate through their online demo environment for thirty days. This speaks to the confidence level that Arena Solutions has in its software and its usability. SAP would never allow this because the difficulty in using SAP could become apparent. Not all companies have an online demo environment like Arena, but still, when a demo is presented the request can be made to have someone from the buyer actually navigate the software under instruction from the presales consultant, or the buyer resource and the presales consultant can take turns running the application. The more usable the application, the more open the vendor will be to getting the maximal exposure to the application for the buyer.

2. There is nothing wrong with allowing a presales consultant to start from a script. There are some things that need to be shown; however, the entire demo should not be from a script. It makes little sense for most of the demo to be "canned" or from a script as the standard things the vendor wants to show should be available for multiple viewings in video format on the vendor's website. At this point, the demo should center on things that the client has asked specifically to see (in advance) and the vendor should have built the demo specifically to answer those questions. Demos can also be made more interactive simply by driving the demo with questions. Presales consultants are under a lot of pressure from the sales team to provide short and smooth demos that leave the buyer with a good impression. However, if it is explained that the buyer does not desire this, typically the demo can be driven differently.

3. Users need to be included in the audience during the demo, and their opinions should be solicited after the demo. Would they personally want to use the software? They should also be told to ask questions whenever they see fit and not at the end of the demo only. Users will pick up on things that executives will not. There is absolutely no logic to exclude the eventual users from a demo. When I worked at i2 Technologies, I recall that on one account the presales and sales team convinced the potential customers to keep users out of the demos. The sales and presales team explained to me that they knew the particular software they were showing was weak and that they would not be able to answer users' questions, so they needed to, in their words, *"sell directly to the top."*

4. Demos should be lengthened. A demo lasting an hour or less, or even multiple demos lasting an hour or less, is not sufficient to really understand how the application works in a variety of circumstances. The shorter the demo, the less representative the demonstration, and the easier it is to cover up weaknesses in the application. After the salespeople and the implementation consultants are gone, what will remain is the software. The software needs to work as the company desires and needs to be able to stand on its own and work efficiently the way the users need it to.

The SAAS/Cloud Vendors versus On-premises Vendors for Long-term Software Evaluation

Most enterprise software that is sold is called "on-premises," meaning that the software is installed on the servers of the buyer and is managed by the buyer. With SaaS/Cloud, the buyer does not actually install any software. Instead, the buyer receives the right to use the software that is installed at the vendor's location. There are a number of advantages and disadvantages to this approach; however one of the major advantages is that companies that offer their software as a SaaS/Cloud solution are in a very good position to offer trials of their software. However, only around 4 percent of all enterprise software is delivered as SaaS at the time of this publication. Some companies like Arena Solutions allow companies to test drive their software for thirty days by logging into their demo environment. However, other SaaS vendors do not offer this service. For instance Data Alliance, an SaaS vendor that I was analyzing recently, chooses to follow the on-premises model of presenting demos to potential clients, even though they could easily provide a SaaS demo environment for companies to test drive at their leisure.

Interpreting the Vendor-presented Story on Integration

Software vendors habitually present integration of the application as simpler and less expensive than it is in reality. This is true of both vendors selling a product that integrates to another product that you already own, or a suite of products from a single vendor that has prebuilt adapters (although not necessarily comprehensive adapters) between the applications to companies that provide point solutions.

Of all the information provided by vendors to software buyers, some of the biggest misrepresentations exist in the portion of the presentation devoted to integration. When I worked for i2 Technologies during the late 1990s, the sales people out of the Singapore office told their clients that XML would handle the integration between the i2 applications and other applications that the company already owned, as well as between i2 applications and applications outside of the company. I spent a good deal of time explaining to executives in i2's Asia client base that XML was just an integration document format, and not an actual integration harness. This was at the height of the XML craze. Then I noticed that the sales team had begun to insert the term "Java API" into sales presentations. API stands for "application programming interface," and this API was written in the Java programming language. Java API was supposedly better than an API written in the C language because it would be platform-independent. The problem was I didn't recall us actually implementing projects with a Java API. It became apparent to me that the integration development group would say anything to sales, and sales seemed to be putting things in the sales presentation slides because the customers responded favorably to our "forward thinking," regardless of whether our product actually worked that way.

If you attempt to dispute how the integration will work in practice, the vendor can always bring in someone more technical than anyone in your IT organization. This person will use a wide range of technical jargon to explain how smoothly your integration will be. It won't and there is little point in debating the point, but evidence indicates that integration will consume about the same amount of resources as it is currently consuming. Another story in the integration pantheon relates to SAP. In sales presentations, SAP misrepresents the comprehensiveness of the adapters they have built between their own products. The executives come out of SAP sales presentations thinking prebuilt adapters cover them if they choose SAP. However, if they were to check the adapters, he or she would find that the adapters do not cover all of the company's requirements.

SAP is a very large enterprise vendor, and many smaller vendors attempt to improve their marketability by becoming "certified" SAP, which amounts to the vendor submitting to the certification process where a minute amount of data is moved between two systems. After the fake test is passed, the vendor gets a certification badge that they can put on their website to improve sales. Outside of the marketing effect, there is little, if any, technical benefit to the implementation as I explain in the article below:

http://www.scmfocus.com/sapintegration/2011/11/15/what-are-saps-vendor-integration-certifications-worth-on-projects/

I have sat through many presentations on applications integration and have heard about all manner of Star Trek-like integration technologies, and yet integration works about the same as it did when I began working in IT consulting many years ago.

Client References

References are important not only for the initial software selection, but also to learn what functionality to enable in applications that are already owned. Vendors will often build functionality into applications that is either never accessed or infrequently accessed by clients because the functionality is not very good or is too high in maintenance.

Following are some of the reasons as to why software vendor references have limited usability.

1. Generally speaking, the vendor will supply only references who are satisfied with the solution (although I have heard of a number of strange stories where the reference provided by a vendor did not implement the software the

vendor said they did, but the vendor still provided the reference). Reviewing vendor references sometimes gives preferential treatment to larger vendors who have more implementations under their belt, and that means more of their functionality has been implemented "someplace."

2. Companies that have agreed to provide references for a vendor typically feel some obligation to that vendor for no other reason than the relationship that they may have with their vendor consultants or vendor account rep. This same interpersonal allegiance is at work when clients co-present with vendors at conferences. Not wanting the vendor to look bad, the client sometimes stretches the truth in terms of how well the software is working. I have personally seen this happen at several conferences where I knew the state of the implementation and it bore no resemblance to what was actually presented.

3. I suppose I am naïve, but I was surprised to learn that vendors and consulting companies may on some occasions pay their references to provide them with a reference.

4. The reference that is provided oftentimes will not have completed their implementation, or the implementation may be so new that the reference account is unsure as to what they actually have. Vendors are quick to declare victory because they know good references can drive sales.

5. Implementing companies are very reticent to admit that a software implementation has gone badly. I am aware of a company that has been implementing two applications for roughly ten years, and has yet to get much functional use from the applications. Therefore, bad implementations are hushed up. However, if software is implemented successfully it is typically discussed openly. Therefore, much like the floor of a casino (where the winning slots make a lot of noise and the losing slots are quiet) the positive observations are greatly over-estimated and over-emphasized.

6. Even if the reference company likes their present software, to what are they compared? This is explained well in an article on software selection. *"Before making a final decision, you should always check vendor references, but take them with a healthy grain of salt. An organization's satisfaction with software depends not only on how well it meets their needs, but how familiar they are with their options—there are a lot of people who are happy*

using difficult, labor-heavy, limited applications simply because they don't know there are better alternatives."—Idealware

However, reference checks can be much better managed and much more useful than they generally are. Rather than asking if the company was happy with software XYZ, it can be more useful to ask how they are using software XYZ. This is much less judgmental and will tend to get to the bottom of how deeply the software is being used. The less judgmental the question, the more likely one is to get to the bottom of what really happened in a software implementation. It can also make sense to prepare a questionnaire that can be sent to the reference in advance. This questionnaire needs to be limited in the number of questions it has, because references cannot be expected to put a great deal of effort into answering these questions.

Implementation Duration Estimation and Project Quality

Software vendors attempt to reduce an application's appearance of risk. Vendors could be an excellent source of information regarding the expected duration of a software project; however, because they are selling software, their information is unreliable. Thus, to reduce a project's risk, the information provided by the vendor must be filtered. Estimates of how long the project will take should not be based on the information provided by the vendor. Instead, benchmarks for projects of the same type should be used. If the project duration is not properly estimated from the beginning (e.g., it is set as too short compared to what is needed), the risk increases because companies have a natural incentive to meet their self-imposed deadlines. And if the time estimate is too short to implement the needed functionality, often they will roll out the application before it is ready and properly tested. A vicious cycle can result, where the company keeps trying to meet successive deadlines (e.g., rolling out the functionality to new regions, or performing new phases of the project, or bringing new functionality within the application online) and there is no time to go back and fix the functionality that was not configured properly in the first place.

One adjustment that can increase the duration's estimation is to break the project into **more** go-lives, which means bringing the application's functionality live in successive waves. The observations and lessons learned from the early go-lives are used to adjust the duration of the successive implementations. Using this method, the scope of the first implementation is small and can be brought up relatively quickly. The company should not adhere strictly to the duration estimate on this first implementation, because the intent is both to bring up functionality as well as to check the discrepancy between the original duration estimate and the duration of the actual implementation.

Which Functionality to Implement First

When you choose the small portion of the overall functionality to implement as your first test, don't stack the odds against yourself. Choose simple functionality that will solve the same problem as well as very complex functionality, and yet will take less time to implement, and that has the higher potential to be implemented successfully. In most cases the software vendor has provided a misimpression as to how difficult the chosen functionality is to implement and maintain.[20]

Traditionally companies implement the more complex technique without first trying the more simple technique, and often they become overwhelmed with the complexity of the solution. Most companies have no idea this is a high-risk approach to system implementation. They simply choose the functionality that appeals to them, and then decide to implement that functionality. They think they are doing the right thing by starting off with the most complex method that hypothetically will deliver the greatest business value. But there are several factors to consider when deciding what functionality to implement and desirability is just one factor. Other factors include the sophistication of the buyer' users and implementation team, the durability of the functionality in question, the funding and timeline of the project as well as several more. Typically, the software vendor will have spent a good deal of time differentiating itself because of its advanced functionality in some area. Thus when the implementation project planning begins, the natural starting point is to implement this complex functionality—this assumption **really needs** to be analyzed. The problem with putting the more complex and advanced functionality in the first implementation/go-live is that the company is not experienced enough with the application to create an accurate implementation duration

---

[20] How much longer depends upon the problem to be modeled and how well the optimizer has been designed by the software vendor.

estimate; they naturally tend to underestimate the duration. As with any topic, the less one knows, the more likely the estimate will leave out important details and result in an underestimation.

Choosing a simple method for the first implementation also allows the company to begin receiving **value** from the application sooner. The users use the application sooner and become familiar with it more quickly. A better-trained group of users is able to support the future rollouts.

However, in most cases, the very opposite of this approach is employed. Most often the implementing company will base its implementation duration estimate on biased estimates from the vendor or the consulting company. The accuracy of the estimate depends greatly upon who provides the estimate.

Who Makes the Initial Estimate?
When I worked for the consulting arm of a software vendor, I routinely had to lengthen the estimate that had been provided by the sales arm of the software vendor. Sales had already made unrealistic estimates of how long the implementation would take. Most of the salespeople had never implemented an application of any kind—much less the one they just sold—and usually pulled the estimates out of thin air. As they would not be performing the implementation personally and wanted only to make the implementation appealing, they had a strong incentive to quote the shortest implementation time frame possible. They got the most money (through the software sale) and left the consulting team with the least amount of money to actually implement the software. After the software was sold, I would come in and say that the estimate needed to be lengthened, which would create friction between the salesperson and myself, and the situation would usually get escalated to the director. The salesperson would typically then say that by me saying to the client that we needed to adjust the time frame of the implementation that I was poisoning the well and putting the relationship in jeopardy. Salespeople are paid to be bold, paid to be optimistic and paid to close deals. The pressure on salespeople to sell is very strong. This is not the group you want projecting project durations—even if they had the implementation experience.

Getting the Estimate from the Right People in the Software Vendor

If the source of a duration estimate is an individual who works against a sales quota and who does not implement for a living, the estimate is **not** reliable. It should go without saying that people without the experience doing the work should not provide duration estimates. For instance, I am often asked to estimate the duration of development work. However, I am not a development manager and have never worked as a developer, so I am not qualified to provide an accurate estimate with respect to software development. And if I do, I put the developer who must do the work in the undesirable position of going back and changing the estimate.

As my previous example shows, a buyer will often receive contradictory estimates depending upon who they speak to within the software vendor organization.[21] As a consulting manager, I was continually asked/pressured by sales to bring down my estimates so as to not "kill the deal." Suffice it to say, this is not a scientific environment within which to make an accurate estimate, and this is why the company must make its **own** estimates without relying upon biased information from the software vendor or the consulting company. Furthermore, while a software vendor may have more knowledge about their application, the buyer has more information about their environment. Many software vendors will say—and I tend to agree with this—that the main factor in implementation duration is the buyer, not the software vendor or the software. Buyers have the knowledge of their internal environment, but consistently underestimate the length of the implementation.

For these reasons I recommend creating an estimate based on a test case. And the best test case is the **first** implementation, which should be a simplified implementation using the simpler methods available within the application and a restricted scope (e.g., restricted by geography, user base, etc.). Once some basic functionality is working and a first go-live has been achieved, the company is in a much better position to estimate the follow-on implementations.

---

[21] Software vendors that do not allow sales to provide project duration estimates will tend to rank higher in the Software Decisions *Quality of Information Provided* criterion.

This approach forces the consultants to produce something in the short term rather than becoming wrapped up in lengthy conversations at the client's expense (who have no experience ever using the application) about the advanced areas of functionality.

Minimizing Risk Through Software Selection

Risk factors change based upon the software category, but also by vendor within the software category. The products of one vendor might be far more difficult to implement than another. This can be determined easily by attempting to con-figure the application oneself. Let's compare two applications with which I have first-hand experience: SAP PP/DS and PlanetTogether Galaxy APS. Galaxy APS is far easier to configure than SAP PP/DS. The master data is easier to change. The more advanced functions are easier to access and simulation capabilities are easier to set up. The two applications not only differ in their speed of implementa-tion (Galaxy APS can be implemented in a number of weeks, rather than a year for PP/DS), but they also have very different risk levels. Because of the design problems with PP/DS, the application is simply a high-risk implementation.

All enterprise software categories are littered with similar examples It is a losing strategy to select software on the basis of a consulting company's recommendation and short demos, although most companies do just that. Companies can easily reduce their IT implementation risk simply by choosing software that is easier to implement.

Conclusion

It should not be news to anyone that information that comes out of sales in any area is often not reliable. This of course also extends to marketing literature. However, there is also an enormous continuum of accuracy along which any vendor can reside. For instance, I have found that when a marketing message comes from SAP it will be either outright false, an exaggeration or a misrepre-sentation of the facts. Because of this, I have to verify the statement through my own research. However, on the other end of the continuum is the example of Arena Solutions, where I have yet to find something inaccurate in their market-ing documentation. However, I can say these things with confidence about both of these software vendors because I have worked with these software vendors for years and read a very large amount of documentation by both companies and have firsthand experience with their applications. When one is new to a software vendor it makes sense to take a skeptical approach to their marketing documentation and statements.

When the topic turns to the software demo, there are all types of simple ways to improve the accuracy of information that is received from a demo that buyers do not take advantage of. The first principle on which the demo should be based is that the demo is entirely for the benefit of the buying company. This means that the buyer has the right to control the demo as they see fit, and to have his or her own people participate in using the application during the demo. Luckily this is an easy matter with modern web conferencing applications where various people can take control of the computers that are presenting. Demos have well-known limitations, the easiest to understand is that demos provide a small amount of time to the evaluators to actually get exposure to the application. Companies with the weakest applications have the greatest incentives to limit the buyer interaction with the application and have the software selection made on more strategic and abstract grounds. The converse is also true. The vendors with the best software want you to spend more time with their application. One example of this is Arena Solutions. Arena Solutions offers a 30 day free trial of their software, and is happy to sell a single license to a company for roughly $80 per month for one user. They know, that once in the door, their application has a high likelihood of being used, and for more users to ask their management for a license. Software vendors like SAP want a major commitment up front. Once the commitment is made, the buyer's flexibility is greatly limited. I have performed software recovery analysis for many companies for applications that never should have been purchased. However, after so much money has been spent on the software license, as well as the implementation, there is a very strong disincentive to move away from the sunk cost of a bad decision. This is actually a major difference between on-premises versus SaaS vendors. With SaaS vendors there is a much greater incentive to keep their customers satisfied, because a SaaS customer can more easily terminate their software subscription.

Integration is a major area of overemphasis in software selections. First, any application can be made to integrate with any other application, and many pre-built adapters that are marketed by software vendors are often much less than they appear during the sales process. Some software vendors, because of their desire to control the purchases of their clients toward their products have deliberately exaggerated the costs of application integration to clients. In fact, ERP purchases have been greatly justified by the desire to reduce integration costs. However, as is explained in the SCM Focus Press book *The Real Story Behind ERP: Separating Fact from Fiction*, the percentage of integration costs that make up IT budgets has not declined after the introduction of ERP systems so the concept of ERP reducing integration costs has been all marketing hyperbole. The primary objective of any software selection should be to get the best application, which can meet the business requirements, not to attempt to save money, for which there is no evidence will be saved, by trying to minimize integration costs with other applications.

Client references sound like an easy way to find out information about how effective the software has been in other accounts. However, in practice client references are tricky. It would be more useful to actually speak to the system's users than the executives, but those resources are generally not made available during a client reference check. How to best manage reference checks to get more accurate information was explained in this chapter.

CHAPTER 9

Evaluating Implementation Preparedness

Implementing companies often are driven to purchase a particular application because it has specific functionality that the company desires. Sometimes the individuals on the software selection team understand the functionality they are purchasing, but often they do not. A great deal of enterprise software is purchased simply because it is trendy at the time; software becomes "hot" at different times and for different reasons. For instance, ERP was a very hot software category prior to the year 2000 because companies were concerned about the Y2K issue in their current systems. Software vendors, consulting companies and their spear-carriers—IT publications and IT analysts—trumped up the Y2K craze to ridiculous proportions.

Y2K drove a great deal of investment in IT, and a great deal of it was wasted. The Y2K issue drove many companies to make unnecessary purchases, and put ERP software vendors in the catbird seat with regard to negotiations. One should really analyze the quality of information that was provided by consulting companies during that time, because it is a heavy indictment of the quality of information one can expect; the advice is clearly entirely wrapped around their revenue model. This important story has been mostly lost; apparently it is not interesting enough for IT journalists or authors to delve into. What is clear from Y2K is that if the major consulting companies could **convince** their clients to buy more of their services to protect their applications against Godzilla, the consulting companies would do it.

As with the fear of Godzilla, consulting companies—along with Y2K vendors—built up the concern to a fever pitch because they knew it would be good for sales. If anyone had bothered to check, several computer science academics at the time stated that the Y2K concern was overblown. However, companies purchasing software tend not to check with academics, but instead get their information from all of the entities covered in this book, as well as books and publications.

Implementation Company Preparedness

It is shocking that so little time is spent on the evaluation of implementation company preparedness for a particular technology, because companies (and departments within companies) vary greatly in their ability to absorb and properly implement new applications. However, while this issue is not raised prior to implementation, it is **quickly** brought up on many implementations after the go-live. Users are frequently blamed for not understanding the system, and blaming users is a universal and favorite activity on the part of IT (although this is often used as a political cover for the executives within the company who made the software selection decision).

Let us ponder this for a moment. Whose job is it to determine if the users were ready for the application? Management. If the users are not prepared for an implementation, there is little reason to proceed with the implementation until they are, so why not check before the fact by getting their input into the process and by observing them using a demonstration version of the system to be acquired?

One of the great myths in enterprise software is that one can simply train one's way to preparedness. Often training, and, in particular, just software training is not sufficient. Software vendors have a strong tendency to provide the impression that the only training necessary is training in their software. However, if the users don't have a sufficient foundation in the subject matter that underpins the software, software specific training will be less successful. Furthermore, new software tends to be more complex than the software it replaces. This means the users must be more skilled. There may be eventually fewer users, but typically not immediately after go live. Several software vendors I am aware of tell the buyer during the sales process that they should be able to cut headcount. I have seen this claim made by software vendors that clearly know from previous implementations that this is not the case. Furthermore, the new software may require the company to hire new individuals because no one internally is suitable or sufficiently experienced in how the new software works and this is an added expense to consider. Of course, buyers could also make application usability a high priority in the software selection process.

Data Management Preparedness

User preparedness is just one factor in a company's preparedness. Any new system relies upon data from other systems. Thus a company's existing systems and those that it plans to install, both of which will interact with the new application, are a major factor in determining preparedness.

Furthermore, different applications often have multiple methods of accomplishing the same objectives, as well as a variety of functionality that can be activated or left disabled. Even after an application is selected, there is a further preparedness question: the company may be prepared fully for one "flavor" of the implementation, is it prepared for another flavor?

How to Perform a Preparedness Analysis

The preparedness of the department that will be using the application is a major factor that affects the risk and probability of success of an implementation. In order to perform and analyze a department's preparedness, it is necessary to have the following domain expertise.

1. *Capable of Performing User Evaluation:* Understand the capabilities and knowledge of the people who will be using the application.

2. *An Understanding of the Application's Capabilities:* Understand the current and planned capabilities of the applications that will interact with the application to be implemented.

3. *An Understanding of the Application's Complexity:* Understand the application, how complex or easy various areas of functionality are to bring up.

4. *An Understanding of Software Category Implementation History:* Understanding the history of implementations of the application at other companies.

The software vendor is in the best position to evaluate preparedness. And if asked directly, a consultant from a software vendor may provide some guidance in this area. This request should be placed to the consultant himself or herself, and not routed through the account management representative. The only way to get an accurate answer is if the answer does **not impact** the sales for the software vendor. Thus it is better if the salesperson never hears of it. If the salesperson catches wind of this initiative, he or she will pressure the consultant to offer a rosy scenario and the analysis will be worse than useless.

Very rarely do implementing companies ask themselves the question of preparedness. Rarely does the implementing company ask its consultants directly to provide advice regarding its preparedness for various functionalities. Instead the implementing company will simply ask for what **they want**. At the beginning of a project, the implementing company has mostly drunk the Kool-Aid. Actually, let's be more specific; they were offered many different Kool-Aid concoctions, and they preferred the Kool-Aid sold by the sales team of a particular vendor.[22] However, the "sexy" functions they heard about in the sales phase may not be the right functionality to bring online for the company nor the right functionality to bring online immediately. This is one of the easiest areas of risk management to address, but it does mean dashing hopes. In essence the sales phase must be looked at as a **different thing altogether** from the implementation phase. Now that the salespeople are gone, the implementing company should have consultants from the software vendor on-site, or at least have access to them. Not everything that was promised by the software vendor's salespeople is going to be attainable.

---

[22] This analogy does not hold universally. Often those that actually implement and use the application preferred a different application, but were overruled by the executive decision-makers. For instance, IT may have put their weight behind a solution because it was consistent with their internal needs, even though the business users did not like the application (a very frequent occurrence). I am oversimplifying in order to focus on how companies go about determining which functionality will be implemented.

The people who do know what is attainable (the consultants from the software vendor), now need to do an evaluation and let the client know what is doable and when it can be accomplished. Unfortunately, the more common approach is to hold the consultant's feet to the fire for the promises made by the salesperson. While this approach may feel gratifying, it will increase the risk of the project greatly. The consultant cannot give you something that does not exist, and putting off reality will simply distract the project from what can be accomplished.

The assessment of the software vendor's consultants will probably sting as expectations must be lowered, but the consultants are going to do the actual work of configuring and designing the solution, and estimates for anything should be taken from those who will actually perform the work.

Who Can Perform Preparedness Evaluations?

I use my work experience to consider whether a consulting company can perform a preparedness evaluation. While some small boutique consulting firms may be able to do this, I don't think the vast majority of consulting companies could be relied upon to provide unbiased information. The consulting partners simply intervene too heavily in the determination of readiness. Generally speaking, the only time that a consulting company will bring up the topic of preparedness is when they have a preference to **not** perform the implementation of the particular software. A consulting company's sales goals are too powerful and the pressure to get more billing hours overwhelms any content expertise that the consulting company may have.

Within software vendors there is a demarcation between sales, marketing, consulting and development. As I have said, you can get the straight story once the salespeople leave. In consulting companies this demarcation does not exist. The more senior members of the consulting company perform the sales and they control what information is released to the client.

If for whatever reason an accurate preparedness evaluation is not obtainable from the software vendor's consultant, one can check the market for **independent consultants**. However, the problem is that independent consultants for the less popular applications are not very common. LinkedIn is a good place to find an independent consultant. One could use a recruiter if pressed for time, but a substantial premium will be paid if an intermediary is used.

Conclusion

One of the biggest, and often un-discussed, risks in enterprise software implementation is buyers that implement software they do not have a good understanding of. The less the buyer knows, the more the software vendor and the consulting company can control the implementation. This is a major reason why at Software Decisions, we provide a rating of the quality of information that is provided—which is a composite score of information from marketing, sales, consulting and development. The less well a buyer understands a software category the less they are able to ascertain their preparedness for an implementation of an application from within that software category. And it is the rare software vendor or consulting company that will tell a buyer to scale back their implementation, as it means reducing one's revenues. Research can help a buyer understand an independent consultant can perform its preparedness, and this—but it is very important that the executive decision makers within the company be ready for the input from the consultant. I have been in this position myself, and have told companies that they should scale down their implementation, and there is often pushback on this information because they are tantalized by the promises of what they hypothetically could attain in terms of benefits if they implemented an application in its most complex form.

CHAPTER 10

Using TCO for Decision Making

Developing the TCO estimations is the difficult part. The more interesting part is actually using the TCO, as there are many varied uses. TCO can be used specifically or generally. For instance, once one has a handle on TCO for an application area, the TCO can be used to make future decisions after the purchase has been made. This is best explained with an example, and one came up while I was writing this book.

Example: TCO and Continuous Improvement
I was developing a proposal for an audit of an application that was already installed and live. This audit was designed to offer areas of improvement in the application. To provide some context, the following text was used on one of the slides from my proposal presentation:

> *"In software implementation, much of the focus is on the initial acquisition and the implementation. However, the measurement of optimal usage and received benefits can be a tricky proposition. To do this requires seeing the application in a variety of environments, and comparing the configuration and planning the outcomes. The audit provides*

important feedback toward the software implementation's current usage and potential areas of improvement.

1. *Some functionality may not be working exactly as desired.*

2. *An unknown feeling as to how much and/or well the investment in the application is being leveraged.*

3. *Issues with, or concerns that, the application may not be optimally integrated (both technically and process–wise) to the other applications in the company."*

Many companies are interested in such an audit if produced by an objective source. However, the question of the price eventually comes up, and while a consulting rate can be fiddled with, the biggest issue is the duration of the audit project. Previous audits/evaluations I had performed typically ranged from one week to three weeks. However, those who wanted a shorter audit based their logic upon the idea that the cost would be too high, as the audit would cost between $12,832 and $14,560. There was no way that some of the companies that had spent roughly $100,000 for both the software and the implementation (this was inexpensive enterprise software) would be willing to spend what could be close to $15,000 for an audit—or what amounted to **fifteen percent** of the total cost of the software and implementation.

However, the problem with this way of thinking is that the cost of the software license and implementation is **not the company's TCO** for the life of the application and therefore should not serve as the estimation of its investment. The TCO studies at Software Decisions show that the software and implementation costs for the application in question represented only about 30 percent of the application's TCO. Other costs included hardware and maintenance. We can estimate the TCO for customers who spent $100,000 for just the software and implementation (consulting), and this is done in the following spreadsheet.

Audit Project Estimate

Consulting Costs

Rate Assumption 1				*Rate Assumption 2*		
Hourly Rate	$	180		Hourly Rate	$	156
Hour Estimate				Hour Estimate		
Straight Time	$	68		Straight Time	$	68
Part Time	$	4		Part Time	$	4
Billing	$	12,960		Billing	$	11,232
Travel Cost	$	1,600		Travel Cost	$	1,600
Total Cost	$	14,560		Total Cost	$	12,832

Typical PT Customer's Overall Expenditure (License & Consulting)	$	100,000			$	100,000

*Based upon Software Decisions analysis of this application. Audit should be justified on the percentage of their overall expenditure for the application.

Other Costs	$	333,333			$	333,333
Total/TCO	$	433,333			$	433,333

Audit as Percentage of Overall Total Cost of Ownership	3.4%		3.0%

From this analysis, it does not seem as if the company should be so concerned about the audit's cost. The cost of an audit is not 15 percent of the customer's cost, but would be between 3% and 3.4% of the application's TCO.

This is a far more logical context within which to make a decision about seeking advice about a solution. Of course, this says nothing about the quality of the audit; this TCO analysis simply provides a context within which to perform the cost-benefit analysis. The audit can provide good results or bad results depending upon the knowledge level and incentives of the individuals performing the audit.

After TCO is developed, it can be put to use in supporting decision-making in a variety of ways, as shown in the example above. Companies should really have TCO analyses performed for all of their applications. It is quite common for companies to make decisions to extend use of their ERP system in some area, usually functionality that is known to be mediocre; however, the decision is driven by the desire to "*get more value from our ERP system*" or to "*leverage our ERP invest-ment.*" These can seem like desirable goals, until one begins to look through the lens of TCO. When executives state that they want to leverage ERP by utilizing more of that ERP system's functionality, exactly what is being leveraged should be understood. In fact, the only thing that is being leveraged is the software license fee, possibly some hardware cost and support fee—but not the implementation costs, some of the hardware cost, and not overall maintenance cost.[23] However, if the hardware cost is taken at a 50 percent value (which either way is a minor portion of the TCO), then the average costs for the license fee, hardware costs, and the support fee across a wide variety of applications come to roughly **15 percent** of the TCO of any new application implementation. And this means not using an application, which would win in a software selection, rather this is simply using the application that happens to be "around."

Overall, "*leveraging*" any current software, be it ERP or other software that the company owns, will not typically save the company more than 15 percent of the TCO of the functionality in that area. Depending upon the situation, there can be more integration costs.[24] However, while the company saves roughly 15 percent on the TCO of the new functionality/application, making this decision will, in most cases, greatly reduce the ROI of the initiative.

Reducing ROI Through Lowered Functionality

How easy is it to reduce the ROI on a software project by at least 15 percent? By using software that is not particularly adept in an area compared to competing options, not only is it easy—it is almost assured. According to statistics that are commonly quoted, software implementations have a success rate of roughly 50 per-cent depending upon how the question in the survey is asked. By our estimates,

---

[23] The support fee paid to the vendor on a yearly basis is only one small component of the maintenance costs.

[24] This greatly depends upon what the integration is with the present solution. Applications from the same vendor are often much less integrated than appears in the sales presentation. Furthermore, most best-of-breed vendors have quite a bit of experience, and often adapters that can connect to, particularly, the more popular ERP systems. But pre-written adapters from both ERP companies and best-of-breed vendors are uniformly overestimated in sales presentations versus their actual on-project performance. If you are interested in an example of a detailed explanation of how much a pre-written adapter can differ from what is presented in the sales process, see this article: http://www.scmfocus.com/sapplanning/2011/05/19/why-i-no-longer-recommend-using-the-cif/.

this is too high, for several good reasons. Some companies that deem the solution to be a success do not know the software area well enough to know how little the application offers over previous approaches to solving the same problem. Off the top of my head I can recall a number of projects where the application does very little to improve on the previous solution, but that truth is hidden from the client by the consulting company or by their own IT department. The business users know, but the executives—who mostly fill out the success/failure question-naires—would not know.

So, trying to save 15 percent on the cost of the implementation with absolutely no consideration for the potential ROI (which is the dominant approach to software selection and decision making in US companies) is one of many factors that keep the success rate of IT implementations so low, and probably lower than the com-monly quoted statistics would lead one to believe. In fact, with IT implementa-tions as risky as they are, the **implementing company needs every possible advantage it can get, and trying to save 15 percent in what is just one category of costs is not the way to do it**. Choosing the best application for the job is the first step in increasing the likelihood of a project's success.

The End Result of Not Using TCO to Inform Decision Making

Deciding to leverage what is *"already purchased"* (a misleading term as it should be rephrased as leveraging what is *"already 15 percent purchased"*) will most often mean taking a **major hit in functionality** and in the ability of the users to perform the activities in the system that the company is asking them to per-form. Furthermore, this line of thinking assumes that all other costs—that is the other 85 percent of costs—are roughly equivalent. However, they are anything but equivalent. On a direct functionality-to-functionality basis, ERP systems are the most expensive systems to implement and to maintain. This is demonstrated by the TCO studies at Software Decisions. ERP systems are almost always combined with **customization,** estimates range from 87 to 93 percent of ERP implementa-tions have from moderate to extensive customization. This customization lengthens out the implementation timeline, which results in increased implementation costs and higher long-term maintenance costs.[25] This is a primary reason why so many

---

[25] Estimations and sources related to the customization burden of ERP systems can be found in *The Real Story Behind ERP: Separating Fact from Fiction.*

companies have continued to implement uncompetitive functionality in their ERP systems when so many better solutions were available in the marketplace, they are attempting to utilize their pre-existing investment in their ERP system. However, research at our companion site Software Decisions demonstrates that this is a faulty logic as companies can only expect to save 12.5 percent of the application's TCO by leveraging the sunk cost of a previously implemented ERP system. [26] Other applications that are specifically designed to meet business requirements (a.k.a. best-of-breed) have better ratings in a variety of compensating criteria. Because of this, it is a simple matter to exceed this cost savings with an increased likelihood of the following:

1. A Longer Implementation

2. More Customization Expense

3. A Higher Risk Implementation

4. Lower Functionality/Worse Fit of Functionality

5. Lower Usability

6. Lower Maintainability

---

[26] This website can be viewed at http://www.softwaredecisions.org.

CHAPTER 11

The Software Decisions' Risk Component Model

To manage risk, it is important to define the most important components of risk that an enterprise software implementation is likely to face and then focus attention on these components. It is also important to properly define "risk." Defining risk is not always as straightforward as it may appear, as is explained in the following quotation.

> *"If a program is behind schedule on releases of engineering drawings to the fabricator, this is not a risk, it is an issue that has already emerged and needs to be resolved and might be complicated. Other examples of issues related to failure of components under test or analysis show a design shortfall. This practice tends to mask true risks, and it serves to track rather than resolve or mitigate risk."*
>
> — Software Risk Management.

I find the way that risk is discussed on projects to be nonsensical. Often the company will go through a list of open issues, list the risk, and then specify the risk-mitigating approach. However, the risks listed tend to be quite tactical in nature. Typical risks on a list like this are: "Development team will not finish in time" and "Not hearing back on workaround from the software vendor." The entire exercise makes it appear as if the **project team** mitigates the most important risks.

Meanwhile, the risks to the project were, for the most part, determined by the executive decision-makers. The risks of listening to the wrong advisor, or buying from the wrong vendor, or using the wrong consulting company are the risks that will have the greatest impact on the overall risk of the project as they essentially define the severity of the risks that will follow. Never I have seen "the executives have not touched enterprise software in fifteen years and have no idea what they are buying" or "the consulting company we are relying upon for objective advice is not a fiduciary and has no legal requirement to place the client's interests ahead of their own" listed as risks on any of these lists.

I once worked with a client who was transitioning to a suite of software that was completely inappropriate for them and would never improve their operations over their current software. They had placed a number of posters around their office that made promises of efficiency improvement resulting from the implementation of the software that they had no hope of ever realizing.

This software was recommended by a major consulting company that never analyzed the client's business requirements—and did not much care what the business requirements of their clients were—and instead recommended the software that they were familiar with implementing. Throughout the project we had risk meetings where we went over tactical risks of the type I have already mentioned. The project management and executive leadership at the client felt good that they were "mitigating risk." However, no matter how many tactical risks they mitigated, the outcome of the project had been set when they picked the wrong software and the wrong consulting company. No tactical risk management can overcome poor decision-making on the part of executives. The executives at this company did not understand the software they purchased and were never in any position from a knowledge perspective to make a good decision. As an example, this company used a single forecasting method (although a highly flexible forecasting method) in the system they were migrating from, which they wanted to use in the new system. Quite some time after they purchased the system, they realized the forecasting method did not exist in the new system. At that point, they added as a project risk the fact that the new forecasting system did not have this forecasting method (which happened to be a very complex forecasting method)! I have to be so bold as to ask: Is this actually a risk, or a mistake of software selection that has been magically transformed into a risk?

Defining the Components of Risk

No risk component model can account for **every risk** on every enterprise software project. Furthermore, it does not make sense to focus on every risk, and the most important risks deserve the most attention.

At Software Decisions, we rate enterprise software project risk on the following factors. Some of these factors are related to the application and vendor, and others are related to the other parties involved in an implementation.[27]

Application-related Risk Categories

1. *Functionality*

2. *Implement-ability*

3. *Usability*

4. *Maintainability*

Vendor-related Risk Categories

1. *Quality of Information Provided*

2. *Implementation Capabilities*

3. *Support Capabilities*

4. *Internal Efficiency*

5. *Current Innovation Level*

---

[27] This website can be found at http://www.softwaredecisions.org

Project- and Client-related Risk Categories

1. *Complexity of Specific Functionality to be Implemented*

2. *Complexity of Specific Installation (number of languages, number of instances, number of teams supporting instances, etc.)*

3. *Preparedness of External Implementing Entities*

4. *Preparedness of the Buyer's Implementation Team*

The Software Decisions website produces ratings for the Application-related and Vendor-related Risk Categories as a self-service offering. This is performed as a starting point for determining the risk of the entire project. Buyers can use this risk estimation as a starting point to complete the risk estimate for client-specific risks, or can have Software Decisions complete the estimate, including an interview and analysis of the rest of the Project- and Client-related Risk Categories.

We assign each application a specific combined application and vendor risk, which is simply the likelihood of success versus the likelihood of failure. Assigning a likelihood of failure is actually quite unusual. However, it allows buyers to understand the risk profile of the applications they are evaluating, and of course, to stay away from those applications with a higher risk. As long as the present method of assuming an identical risk level for all applications and all vendors remains the standard, buyers will continue to buy high-risk application (and applications with a risk higher than they had any idea they were purchasing).

This risk estimate is an aggregated calculation from multiple application and vendor criteria to which we assigned values. Our final risk value is not simply a straight average of all the input components, but rather is a **weighted average** as we have found some components to be more critical—even among this important group—than other risk factors.

The description of these risk categories follows listed below.

Application Related Risk Categories Descriptions

Functionality

This is the potential of the application's functionality to match the business process, as well as the reliability of the functionality. This is itself a composite score because it includes one score for functionality quality, and one for functionality scope.

The scores at the Software Decisions website provide detail on each application in terms of how well it scores for each subcategory of functionality. While many vendors (larger software vendors in particular) would prefer if people believed that functionality scope trumped functionality quality, this is not borne out in our studies of actual projects. One of the most important lessons learned about enterprise software is that just because the release notes or marketing literature talks about an application containing specific functionality, does not mean that the functionality is equal to the same functionality of other vendors. This sounds completely obvious; in fact I cringe somewhat when writing this statement as it is so elementary. However, I feel it's necessary to discuss this point because many companies behave as if functionality between applications is equal.

Determination of the application functionality score is based upon a detailed analysis of the application in terms of its **real ability** to leverage functionality. It also means making value judgments as to how frequently the functionality can actually be put into action.

Implement-ability

Any application can be given a score that reflects how easily it can be implemented. There are many factors that go into such an "implement-ability" score. One factor is master data parameter maintenance; another is how hard it is to configure the application. Generally speaking, implement-ability of an application is not measured, but it is in fact measurable.

Some of the lowest scoring applications in terms of implement-ability are Tier 1 ERP systems and BI Heavy applications, and it's not surprising that they tend to have the longest implementation timelines in enterprise software. Older applications also tend to be less implementable than newer applications. SaaS applications are more implementable generally than those delivered on-premises. This is due to several factors, a very important one being that much of the complexity of setting up and maintaining the hardware for the application is taken care of. The more control the software vendor has over the application, the better the implement-ability, which is why SaaS scores so well in this regard.

Usability

Users gravitate naturally to applications that rank high in usability. These applications require less training and are inherently easier to understand and troubleshoot when things go wrong, even if the complexity of what the application does under the covers is high. Highly usable applications don't need to be forced on users, as users naturally want to access them in order to do their jobs more efficiently.

At Software Decisions, we sometimes rate applications by using the applications ourselves. Other times we request that the software vendor demonstrate menus and functionality that we then compare against other applications. We do not adjust or normalizes the usability factor per software category, as we think this would be confusing. As such, some software categories tend to have higher or lower average usability than other software categories.

Maintainability

The maintainability score is related to the implement-ability score, but looks at longer-range factors. Applications differ drastically on the basis of maintainability, and the maintainability of an application greatly affects its total cost of ownership or TCO. According to the TCO analysis database at Software Decisions, roughly 60 percent of an application's TCO is related to its maintenance costs. Of all the costs, maintainability is the largest cost, but probably the least emphasized. And while other costs tend to be front loaded toward the beginning of the buyer's interaction with the application, maintenance costs run until the system is decommissioned.

Descriptions of Vendor-related Risk Categories

The vendor-related risk categories rate the vendor across the criteria that are considered the most important for choosing a software vendor. Enterprise software purchases create a long-term relationship between the buyer and the vendor, and therefore the vendor should be a highly emphasized criterion in a software selection.

Generally speaking, application quality and vendor quality are strongly related to one another—but not always. If an application scores high but the vendor scores low, this is usually because the application was acquired. An application that scores low while the software vendor scores high is usually because the application is not within the core of what that vendor does.

The Quality of Information Provided

At Software Decisions, an overall score is calculated for the quality of information provided by the software vendor. Enterprise software vendors differ greatly in the quality of information they provide to customers. Factors that influence the quality of information provided by the software vendor's salespeople include:

- The sales approach

- How the software vendor motivates and compensates its salespeople

- How well their salespeople know the application

- How much their market is saturated versus the number of resources they deploy into sales

The quality of an application's documentation depends upon the emphasis that the software vendor puts into developing anything from their user manuals to their marketing literature. We give our best compliments to software vendors when they are either thought leaders in their space, or they make a genuine effort to educate with their documentation. Another factor that influences the score given for the quality of information is how clear the messaging is from the software vendor. Some vendors are better able than others to explain what their application does and how it can be used.

Implementation Capabilities

The large software vendors tend to outsource most of their consulting—in exchange for being recommended by the major consulting companies. Therefore, the role of the implementation consultant for a large software vendor becomes, in part, to support the major consulting company's implementation resources in addition to providing value to the end client.

Smaller software vendors tend to staff much more of the overall external implementation team. Many factors work into how effective the software vendor's implementation capabilities are, including how long the vendor's consultants have worked for the software vendor, their motivation, and the internal fairness of the software vendor with respect to how they treat their employees.

Another factor—frequently overlooked—is how much **authority** the consulting team has versus the sales group. In many software vendors, the sales division is simply far **too** powerful in relation to consulting or implementation. This is the kind of statement that will immediately get me accused of bias by experienced salespeople, as I am an implementation resource myself and have never worked in sales. However, if the sales division holds some power over the consulting or implementation team, it means that information provided by the consulting arm will be censored. This is done so that information provided by the consulting arm is in line with earlier false information used by sales to close the sale. While this may help the software vendor get the sale, it's hard to see how this is good for the buyer by any logic. As I often say, as much as we try to prevent its occurrence, eventually reality happens.

This topic is covered in the following article.

http://www.scmfocus.com/sapprojectmanagement/2011/07/what-is-an-sap-platinum-consultant/

Support Capabilities

Obviously, support is a very important measurement of any software vendor. However, the only place we see this measured is at crowdsourcing sites such as G2 Crowd.

Support is the horse's mouth on the software after the implementation is live; support has human resources with many years of experience in the application and will be the go-to source when the buyer's internally trained resources cannot figure out the answer.

It should be understood that poorly designed software cannot be overcome with effective support. Poorly designed software is a losing situation even if a great deal is invested in support, because support is so expensive to supply. This is why software selection using the criterion of maintainability is so important. When an application is well designed, the vendor support personnel can figure out what is wrong more quickly.

Internal Efficiency

There are enormous differences between various software vendors in terms of their internal efficiency, and in my experience, internal efficiency is inversely related to their level of bureaucracy. I visited or worked in many software companies, and the feeling is very different depending upon the particular vendor. Smaller and highly innovative software vendors are fun places to work; even across different software categories, they have a similar feel to them. Meetings tend to be kept to a minimum (except for the senior members) and they tend to have an informal feel about them. Larger software vendors have lost much of this culture, and, in fact, employ more conservative individuals (conservative individuals tend to be attracted to the stability offered by the large vendor) and the conversations tend to orbit much more around business than around software.

It is no big secret that as companies grow, they become more bureaucratic and their efficiency goes down. They make up for this with market power. However, market power helps only with marketing and gaining acceptance for an application, not with things that actually support development or implementations. Mega-vendors, like SAP and Microsoft, have a lot of difficulty in innovating; I consider them more as marketing entities and stewards of software that was developed or purchased some time ago, rather than as originators of anything new.

However, while there is strong correlation between vendor size and bureaucracy, bureaucracy is not identical for all vendors of a similar size, and some small vendors have a shocking amount of bureaucracy.

Something that is generally not discussed (but really should be) is the significant cost imposed on customers by the software vendor due to bureaucracy. Once a buyer implements an enterprise software application, the company is **quite** dependent upon the software vendor for support, upgrades, training, etc. When a software vendor tends toward more bureaucracy, questions take longer to get answered and requests get lost. Who can actually make important decisions on specific topics is increasingly in doubt. Politics ends up determining what answers are received rather than what is technically true or false.

I have experience working with both high and low efficiency software vendors, and the differences are stark. For this reason I consider the bureaucracy level of software vendors to be one of the most underestimated risks and costs of software selection. Interestingly, I have never once seen bureaucracy listed as a criterion for any software selection exercise by **any** major consulting company—perhaps because they rate very highly in bureaucracy themselves.

Current Innovation Level

All software vendors go through a lifecycle: they are small and innovative and then they tend to calcify and become more marketing and financially driven entities while their development productivity drops significantly. At the end of their lifecycle, they may do almost no innovation and instead spend most of their energies in marketing, acquisitions, and in chasing their tails in bureaucracy and management intrigue. Therefore, determining the current innovation level for software vendors is important for corporate buyers because enterprise software is a long-term commitment. Even SaaS application purchases, which hypothetically can be cancelled within a month, still have significant lock-in due to costs for transferring to a new application (retraining, data migration, becoming comfortable with a new software vendor, etc.).

Typically a buyer will use any enterprise application for at least seven years, and normally the buyer will upgrade throughout the lifetime of the application. Therefore, the buyer is purchasing not only the software in its present state, but also in its future state. The current innovation level rating provides the buyer with an idea of the future potential of the software vendor's applications. We do not take into account the historical level of a software vendor's innovation because this cannot be used to project the future. As stated, software vendors go through a lifecycle of innovation, where they are very innovative in the beginning, and less and less innovative as time goes on. The software vendor's innovation level in previous years is not relevant to its predicted level of future innovation.

Description of Project- and Client-related Risk Categories

The Complexity of Specific Functionality to Be Implemented
Applications in every enterprise software category can be implemented using any amount of its functionality; however, it's incorrect to assume, as many do, that all functionality must be implemented at the outset. Accessing more advanced areas of functionality increases project risk in at least three ways. First, the functionality itself is more complex, which tends to mean the functionality is less reliable. Second, complex functionality can stretch the skill level of the consultants. Third the complex functionality can be more difficult for users and decision-makers to understand.

The Preparedness of External Entities
Outside of software vendors, it is difficult to obtain good consulting support. Generally speaking, the major consulting companies only have resources that are trained in the software from the largest vendors—which is why they continually recommend software from the largest vendors. Keeping a bench of consultants trained on five of the major applications in any one software category would be a challenge, and the likelihood that one resource would come available when the opportunity presents itself would be less likely. For this reason, the large consulting companies prefer to support as few applications as possible, and typically

only specialize in a few brands—normally the same brands across the various software categories.

One easy way to improve the overall preparedness of the implementing company is to add more consultants from the software vendor rather than from consulting entities. On average, consultants from software vendors add far more value to an implementation than do consultants from consulting companies. Many projects have run into problems in part because the consulting company partner was overly focused on **maximizing** its billing hours by replacing better-qualified vendor consultants with its own consultants. As a result, the project team lacked the skills to work effectively.

Software vendors have the advantage over consulting firms in providing value. Vendors know the software better and typically they are **less** focused on maximizing billing hours as they make more of their money from software sales. They have a higher incentive than any consulting company to get the software live (so they can use the client as a reference account for future software sales). This is doubly advantageous because unlike consulting companies, software vendors charge a lower billing rate and have no incentive to stretch out the project.[28]

The Preparedness of the Buyer's Implementation Team
The buyer must assign the right resources for the right amount of time. Assigning internal resources to the internal team who still have some of their regular job responsibilities is one of the biggest issues with a software implementation.

---

[28] However, sometimes the consulting company will state that without a certain number of its own consultants it can't "guarantee the project." I recall IBM once say this, basically as a mini tantrum for not getting their way on a project. However, one should recognize that no consulting companies provide guarantees. Check the consulting contract; the consulting company is obligated only to provide consulting services in some good faith capacity. Even on fixed price implementations, consulting companies have all types of tricks for getting clients to sign off on milestones that have not actually been met. Essentially, unless something outrageous happens, the consulting company has no real legal liability. Also any project complaint from a senior member of any major consulting company on any topic can be neatly translated into, *"This does not maximize my billing hours and allow me to meet my quota."*

Conclusion

As was stated earlier, these are not all of the risk factors, but we consider them the most important ones. For example, notice that we have no category for "The Preparedness of the Buyer's IT Department." Typically all buyers' IT departments will be able to install the software, patch software, acquire the hardware, etc., and so we don't rate this risk factor highly. However, if the IT department is performing the implementation (which occasionally happens if the buyer has hired IT personnel with the necessary implementation experience), this simply moves over to the category of "The Preparedness of External Implementing Entities." The IT department is now acting as the consulting entity. In that case, their preparedness must be evaluated.[29]

---

[29] While this is just an example, it should be stated that we have not seen this scenario work very well. IT departments tend to be better at maintenance and new application implementation. The decision to use the IT department to implement the application can be driven by a desire to save money, but will often result in a poor match of skills. At one client with whom we consulted, they hired an experienced consultant who had related skills, but no experience with the application. This consultant took a lower compensation as a full-time employee, implemented the software very poorly, used this experience to build his resume, and then left the company before the go-live. He did this because the implementation had zero chance of success as he had no idea what he was doing and he needed to leave before it all came crashing down. This was an example of being penny wise but pound foolish in terms of resourcing the project. One of the reasons consultants are paid more is because they can offer the exact skill desired (and they can be quickly replaced if they do not fit the bill). Independent consultants offer a far better value and are better at reducing sticker shock. However, they must be found directly through sources such as LinkedIn. If one goes to a recruiter, there will be some cost savings versus obtaining them from a consulting company, but not very much.

CHAPTER 12

Conclusion

Companies that implement enterprise software have many areas where they can improve their management of risk. The first place to start was discussed in Chapter 2, where six of the primarily flawed strategies for risk management with respect to enterprise software were introduced. Several of these strategies are based upon assumptions that have no evidence to support them, but are propagated by entities that financially benefit from having buyers believe the assumptions be to true. One of the most important steps in improving risk management is debunking these myths regarding risk management.

The enterprise software market is not an easy market within which to make a decision. First, enterprise software is, in most cases, the most complex product that any company purchases. Buyers are dependent upon information that is gleaned from both software vendors salespeople as well as consulting companies, both of which have conflicts of interest in providing the complete picture. The enterprise software market is not regulated. These issues are discussed in Chapter 4. This chapter brought up the common requirements for an efficient market, and found that the enterprise software market is lacking in all of them.

This is what happens when a market is unregulated, and also makes enterprise software selection and risk management much more difficult.

A big part of risk management is determining implementation preparedness. When exposed to the marketing documentation and the sales pitch a large amount of functionality can seem appealing, but bringing complex functionality live and maintaining this functionality is often a lot of work. Secondly, more sophisticated functionality can be less reliable than older, less tantalizing functionality. However, even if the functionality is in working order, preparedness must be determined, and this requires an honest evaluation of the state of the skills, systems, bandwidth and management of the buyer. Preparedness evaluation is a tricky endeavor, because it means admitting the internal limitations of the buyer. It means, if the desire is eventually to implement the functionality, then it means implementing changes and spending money to improve preparedness. Software vendors tend to soft peddle preparedness because it is a downer and negatively correlated with obtaining sales. For most software vendors, whatever the preparedness level of the buyer, is appropriate for implementing their software.

In order to measure risk in a detailed way, at Software Decisions, we created a risk component model that includes application related risk categories, vendor related risk categories and project and client related risks. This is performed as a starting point for determining the risk of the entire project. The reason for doing this is that without risk estimation being performed, companies will continue to underestimate their risks, and lean toward higher risk applications and implementations. Buyers must move beyond relying upon platitudes regarding risk, or thinking that simply identifying and declaring things to be "a risk" if they intend to better manage project risk. Risk management is a combination of strategies that combine validating information sources, choosing implementation partners, software selection, and performing preparedness assessments. Far too often, risk management is something that is considered to begin once an implementation has begun. However, at that point, many of the most important decisions that impact the implementation risk have already been determined. Risk management strategies should be considered as soon as a company begins thinking about investing in new enterprise software.

Other Books from SCM Focus

Bill of Materials in Excel, ERP, Planning and PLM/BMMS Software

http://www.scmfocus.com/scmfocuspress/the-software-approaches-for-improving-your-bill-of-materials-book/

Constrained Supply and Production Planning in SAP APO

http://www.scmfocus.com/scmfocuspress/select-a-book/constrained-supply-and-production-planning-in-sap-apo/

Enterprise Software Risk: Controlling the Main Risk Factors on IT Projects

http://www.scmfocus.com/scmfocuspress/it-decision-making-books/enterprise-software-project-risk-management/

Enterprise Software Selection: How to Pinpoint the Perfect Software Solution using Multiple Information Sources

http://www.scmfocus.com/scmfocuspress/it-decision-making-books/enterprise-software-selection/

Enterprise Software TCO: Calculating and Using Total Cost of Ownership for Decision Making

http://www.scmfocus.com/scmfocuspress/it-decision-making-books/enterprise-software-tco/

Gartner and the Magic Quadrant: A Guide for Buyers, Vendors and Investors

http://www.scmfocus.com/scmfocuspress/it-decision-making-books/gartner-and-the-magic-quadrant/

Inventory Optimization and Multi-Echelon Planning Software

http://www.scmfocus.com/scmfocuspress/supply-books/the-inventory-optimization-and-multi-echelon-software-book/

Multi-Method Supply Planning in SAP APO

http://www.scmfocus.com/scmfocuspress/select-a-book/multi-method-supply-planning-in-sap-apo/

Planning Horizons, Calendars and Timings in SAP APO

http://www.scmfocus.com/scmfocuspress/select-a-book/planning-horizons-calendars-and-timings-in-sap-apo/

Process Industry Manufacturing Software: ERP, Planning, Recipe, MES & Process Control

http://www.scmfocus.com/scmfocuspress/production-books/process-industry-planning/

Replacing Big ERP: Breaking the Big ERP Habit with Best of Breed Applications at a Fraction of the Cost

http://www.scmfocus.com/scmfocuspress/erp-books/replacing-erp/

Setting up the Supply Network in SAP APO

http://www.scmfocus.com/scmfocuspress/select-a-book/setting-up-the-supply-network-in-sap-apo/

SuperPlant: Creating a Nimble Manufacturing Enterprise with Adaptive Planning Software

http://www.scmfocus.com/scmfocuspress/production-books/the-superplant-concept/

Supply Chain Forecasting Software

http://www.scmfocus.com/scmfocuspress/the-statistical-and-consensus-supply-chain-forecasting-software-book/

Supply Planning with MRP, DRP and APS Software

http://www.scmfocus.com/scmfocuspress/supply-books/the-supply-planning-with-mrpdrp-and-aps-software-book/

The Real Story Behind ERP: Separating Fiction from Reality

http://www.scmfocus.com/scmfocuspress/erp-books/the-real-story-behind-erp/

Spreading the Word

SCM Focus Press is a small publisher. However, we pride ourselves on publishing the unvarnished truth, which most other publishers will not publish. If you felt like you learned something valuable from reading this book, please spread the word by adding a review to our Amazon.com page. http://www.amazon.com/Shaun-Snapp/e/B003CY62D0

References

A Brief History of the ERP Problem. CIO. December 20, 2004.
http://www.cio.com/article/935/A_Brief_History_of_the_ERP_
Problem?page=4&taxonomyId=3009.

Aloini, Davide. Dulmin, Riccardo. Valeria, Mininno. *Risk Assessment in ERP Projects*, University of Pisa, 2009.

Angell, Marcia M.D, *The Truth About the Drug Companies.*
http://www.wanttoknow.info/truthaboutdrugcompanies.

Avdoshin, Sergey M. Pesotskaya, Elena Y. *Software Risk Management.*
Institute of Electrical and Electronics Engineers. April 20, 2012.

Bardach, Eugene. *A Practical Guide for Policy Analysis: The Eightfold Path to More Effective Problem Solving, 4th Edition.* CQ Press College, 2011.

Beheshti M, Hooshang. *What Managers Should Know About ERP/ERP II.* Management Research News, Vol 29, No 4, pp. 184-193, 2006.

Biello, David. *Grass Makes Better Ethanol than Corn Does.* Scientific American. January 8, 2008.
http://www.scientificamerican.com/article/grass-makes-better-ethanol-than-corn/.

Birch, Nicholas. *Why ERP Doesn't Work.* June 2007.
http://www.istart.co.nz/index/HM20/PC0/PVC197/EX27129/AR29697.

Bridgwater, Adrian. *ERP is Dead, Long Live Two-Tier ERP.* December 12, 2012.
    http://www.computerweekly.com/blogs/cwdn/2012/12/erp-is-dead-long-live-two-tier-erp.html.

Calculating the Total Cost of Ownership for Offshoring Manufacturing.
    http://www.operonresource.com/wp-content/themes/operon/assets/pdf/Calc-total-cost-ownership-offshoring.pdf.

Chiappinelli, Chris. *New ERP Paradigm Challenges Old Assumptions.* March 2, 2011.
    http://www.techmatchpro.com/article/2011/3/new-erp-paradigm-challenges-old-assumptions.

Clarke, Gavin. *Larry 'Shared databases are crap' Ellison reveals shared Oracle database.* October 1, 2012.
    http://www.theregister.co.uk/2012/10/01/ellison_oow_2012_database_cloud/.

Columbus, Louis. *ERP Prediction for 2013: The Customer Takes Control.* Forbes. January 7, 2013.
    http://www.forbes.com/sites/louiscolumbus/2013/01/07/erp-prediction-for-2013-the-customer-takes-control/.

Corn Ethanol. Accessed July 3, 2013.
    http://en.wikipedia.org/wiki/Corn_ethanol.

Cullinan, Charles, Sutton Steven G, and Arnold, Vicky. *Technology Monoculture: ERP Systems, "Technology Process Diversity" and the Threat to the Information Technology Ecosystem.* Advances in Accounting Behavioral Research, Volume 13 13–30, 2010.

Depillis, Lyndia. *Meet CGI Federal, the Company Behind the Botched Launch of HealthCare.gov.* The Washington Post. October 16, 2013.
    http://www.washingtonpost.com/blogs/wonkblog/wp/2013/10/16/meet-cgi-federal-the-company-behind-the-botched-launch-of-healthcare-gov/.

Eller, Claudia. *Warner Bros. to Outsource Jobs Overseas.* Los Angeles Times. January 10, 2009.
    http://articles.latimes.com/2009/jan/10/business/fi-warner10.

Elragal, Ahmed and Al-Serafi, Ayman. *The Effect of ERP System Implementation on Business Performance: An Exploratory Case-Study.* October 2011.
    http://www.ibimapublishing.com/journals/CIBIMA/2011/670212/670212.pdf.

Enterprise Resource Planning. Accessed July 23, 2013.
    http://en.wikipedia.org/wiki/Enterprise_resource_planning#Two-tier_enterprise_resource_planning.

Eskilsson, Helene, Nystrom, Christiana and Windler , Maria. *ERP System and Effects: A Comparison of Theory and Practice.* Gotenborg University, 2003.

Fauscette, Michael. *Maintaining ERP Systems: The Cost of Change.* IDC. May, 2013.

Ferreira, John and Prokopets, Len. *Does Offshoring Still Make Sense?* February 2009. http://www.areadevelopment.com/article_pdf/id44472_does-offshoring-still-make-sense.pdf.

Finke, Nikki. *Warner Bros. Announces 800 Layoffs.* January 20, 2009. http://www.deadline.com/2009/01/as-expected-warner-bros-announces-layoffs/.

Greenbaum, Joshua. *Rethinking TCO: Towards a More Viable and Useful Measure of IT Costs.* Enterprise Application Consulting. Spring, 2005.

IT Spending: How Do You Stack Up? Gartner, 2003.

Jacobs, F. Robert and Weston Jr., F.C. *ERP—A Short History.* Journal of Operations Management, 2007.

Kanaracus, Chris. *Air Force scraps massive ERP project after racking up $1 billion in costs.* November 14, 2012. http://www.cio.com/article/721628/Air_Force_scraps_massive_ERP_project_after_racking_up_1_billion_in_costs.

Kimberling, Eric. *Are Two-Tier ERP Systems Finally Becoming Mainstream?* December, 19, 2012. http://panorama-consulting.com/are-two-tier-erp-systems-finally-becoming-mainstream/.

Kimberling, Eric. *Top Ten Predictions for the Global ERP Industry in 2013.* November 20, 2012. http://panorama-consulting.com/top-ten-predictions-for-the-global-erp-industry-in-2013/

MacCormack, Alan. *Evaluating Total Cost of Ownership for Software Platforms: Comparing Apples, Oranges and Cucumbers.* AEI-Brookings Joint Center for Regulatory Studies, 2013.

Mann, Charles. *Why Software Is So Bad.* Technology Review. July 1, 2002. http://www.technologyreview.com/featuredstory/401594/why-software-is-so-bad/.

Manufacturing. Accessed July 12, 2013. https://en.wikipedia.org/wiki/Manufacturing.

Medina, Stephano. *CGI Federal: Here's Why Healthcare.gov is So Screwed Up*. Policy Mic. October 24, 2013.
http://www.policymic.com/articles/69807/cgi-federal-here-s-why-healthcare-gov-is-so-screwed-up.

Moon, Andy. *Are the Rewards of ERP Systems Worth the Risk?* March 27, 2008.
http://www.techrepublic.com/blog/it-news-digest/are-the-rewards-of-erp-systems-worth-the-risk/#.

Opportunity Cost. Accessed June 22, 2013.
https://en.wikipedia.org/wiki/Opportunity_cost.

Overby, Stephanie. *IT Increases Application Outsourcing Despite Disappointing Strategic Value*. July 12, 2013.
http://www.cio.com/article/736275/IT_Increases_Application_Outsourcing_Despite_Disappointing_Strategic_Value.

Overby, Stephanie. *The Hidden Costs of Offshore Outsourcing*. September 01, 2003.
http://www.cio.com/article/29654/The_Hidden_Costs_of_Offshore_Outsourcing.

Pabo-Nazao, Placid and Raymond, Louis. *In House Development as an Alternative for ERP Adoption by SMES: A Critical Case Study*. 17th Information Systems, 2009.

Philips, Steven Scott. *Control Your ERP Destiny*. Street Smart ERP Publications, 2012.

Prouty, Kevin and Castellina, Nick. *To ERP or Not to ERP*. April, 2011.
http://www.plex.com/wordpress/wp-content/uploads/2012/05/Aberdeen-ERPvsNoERP.pdf.

Proving a Negative. Accessed March 15, 2013.
http://en.wikipedia.org/wiki/Proving_a_negative.

Reichman, Andrew. *TCO Is Overrated*. August 26, 2008.
http://www.forrester.com/TCO+Is+Overrated/fulltext/-/E-RES44545?docid=44545.

Rettig, Cynthia. *The Trouble With Enterprise Software*. MIT Sloan. Fall, 2007.
http://sloanreview.mit.edu/article/the-trouble-with-enterprise-software/.

Rohm, Ted. *To ERP or Not to ERP, that is the C-level Question*. February 22, 2013.
http://www.technologyevaluation.com/research/article/To-ERP-or-Not-to-ERP-that-Is-the-C-level-Question.html.

Ruffinatti, Adrián. *Costo Total de Propiedad Estrategias en la Industria del Software*. Amazon Digital Services, 2010.

SAP Best Practices.
   http://help.sap.com/bp_dm604/BBlibrary/General/SAP_Best_Practices_overview_
   EN.pdf.

Schmidt, Marty. *Total Cost of Ownership TCO Explained.* 2004.
   http://www.business-case-analysis.com/total-cost-of-ownership.html.

Single Instance ERPs are Scarce, Says Study. October, 2005.
   http://www.cimaglobal.com/Thought-leadership/Newsletters/Insight-e-magazine/
   Insight-March-2006/Single-instance-ERPs-are-scarce-says-study/.

Sommer, Brian. *ERP's Franken-soft and how Workday avoids it.* November 13, 2012.
   http://www.zdnet.com/erps-franken-soft-and-how-workday-avoids-it-7000007200/.

Snapp, Shaun. *Enterprise Software Selection: How to Pinpoint the Perfect Software
   Solution Using Multiple Information Sources.* SCM Focus Press, 2013.

Snapp, Shaun. *Gartner and the Magic Quadrant: A Guide for Buyers, Vendors and
   Investors.* SCM Focus Press, 2013.

Snapp, Shaun. *Superplant,* SCM Focus Press, 2013.

Snapp, Shaun. *Supply Planning with MRP, DRP and APS Software.* SCM Focus
   Press, 2012.

Snapp, Shaun. *The Bill of Materials, in Excel, Planning, ERP and PLM/BMMS
   Software,* SCM Focus Press, 2013.

Snapp, Shaun. *The Real Story Behind Two-tiered ERP,* SCM Focus Press, 2014.

Standards for High-Quality Research and Analysis.
   http://www.rand.org/standards.html.

Tautology. Accessed June 27, 2013.
   http://en.wikipedia.org/wiki/Tautology_(rhetoric).

The Best of Class Financial System Strategy: An Alternative to ERP Platforms.

Technology Evaluation Centers.

The Decline of Single Instance Big ERP. Why Two-Tier ERP is on the CIO Agenda.
   http://www.netsuiteblogs.com/the-decline-of-single-instance-big-erp-why-two-tier-
   erp-is-on-the-cio-agenda.

Themistocleous, Marinos, Irani, Zahir and O'Keefe, Robert M. *ERP and Application
   Integration: Exploratory Survey.* Business Process Management Journal, Vol. 7
   Iss: 3, pp.195–204.

The Real ROI from i2 Supply Chain Management. Nucleus Research, 2003.

Total Cost of Ownership.
  http://www.gartner.com/it-glossary/total-cost-of-ownership-tco/.

Tzuo, Tien. *The End Of ERP.* February 9, 2012.
  http://www.forbes.com/sites/ciocentral/2012/02/09/the-end-of-erp/2/.

Wailgum, Thomas. *ERP Sticker Shock: Maintenance, Upgrades and Customizations.*
  September 23, 2010.
  http://www.cio.com/article/618117/ERP_Sticker_Shock_Maintenance_Upgrades_
  and_Customizations.

Wailgum, Thomas. *SaaS ERP Has Buzz, But Who Are the Real Players?* March 10,
  2010.
  http://www.cio.com/article/572463/SaaS_ERP_Has_Buzz_But_Who_Are_the_
  Real_Players.

Wailgum, Thomas. *The Problem with Mature ERP Systems.* September 16, 2009.
  http://www.cio.com/article/502280/The_Problem_with_Mature_ERP_Systems

Wailgum, Thomas. *Want to Save $10 Million or More on ERP? Don't Buy Oracle or
  SAP.* February 26, 2009.
  http://blogs.cio.com/thomas_wailgum/want_to_save_10_million_or_more_on_erp_
  dont_buy_oracle_or_sap?source=nlt_cioenterprise

Wailgum, Thomas. *Why ERP Is Still so Hard.* September 09, 2009.
  http://www.cio.com/article/501656/Why_ERP_Is_Still_So_Hard

Wainwright, Phil. *ERP, RIP? Cloud financials and revenue management in 2013.*
  January 4, 2013.
  http://www.zdnet.com/erp-rip-cloud-financials-and-revenue-management-in-2013-
  7000009376/.

Wagner, David. *Old & Bad ERP All Over Manufacturing.* April 17, 2013.
  http://www.enterpriseefficiency.com/author.asp?section_id=1151&doc_id=262241.

Weisenthal, Joe. *Here's the Trend Obama is Fighting, If He Wants to Save American
  Manufacturing.* August 23, 2010.
  http://www.businessinsider.com/chart-of-the-day-manufacturing-employment-as-a-
  percentage-of-total-non-farm-payrolls-2010-8.

What is ERP?
  http://www.netsuite.com/portal/resource/articles/erp/what-is-erp.shtml.

Wolpe, Toby. *When SAP Sprawl Is Cool: Could Cutting Back Your ERP be More Pain Than It's Worth?* May 9, 2013.
http://www.zdnet.com/are-businesses-wasting-millions-on-sap-erp-they-dont-need-7000015133/.

Worthen, Ben. *Extreme ERP Makeover.* December 9, 2003.
http://www.cio.com.au/article/181834/extreme_erp_makeover/?pp=5.

Zhang, Zhe, Lee, Matthew K. O., Zhang, Liang, Huang and Xiaoyuan, Huang. *A Framework of ERP Systems Implementation Success in China: An Empirical Study.* 2004.

Links in the Book

Chapter 1

http://www.scmfocus.com/writing-rules/

http://www.scmfocus.com

http://www.scmfocus.com/scmfocuspress/it-decision-making-books/
enterprise-software-project-risk-management/

Chapter 2

http://www.scmfocus.com/enterprisesoftwarepolicy/2012/03/11/why-
the-largest-enterprise-software-companies-have-no-reason-to-
innovate/

http://www.scmfocus.com/sapplanning/2011/05/19/why-i-no-longer-
recommend-using-the-cif/

http://www.scmfocus.com/softwaredecisions/plans/solution-
architecture-packages/

Chapter 4

http://www.scmfocus.com/enterprisesoftwarepolicy/2012/03/11/why-
the-largest-enterprise-software-companies-have-no-reason-to-
innovate/

http://www.scmfocus.com/enterprisesoftwarepolicy

http://www.softwaredecisions.com

http://www.scmfocus.com/softwaredecisions/santa-clause-syndrome/

http://www.scmfocus.com/softwaredecisions/current-innovation-level/

http://www.scmfocus.com/enterprisesoftwarepolicy/2012/01/27/how-common-is-it-for-sap-to-take-intellectual-property-from-partners/

http://www.scmfocus.com/inventoryoptimizationmultiechelon/2010/01/its-time-for-the-sap-xapps-program-to-die/

Chapter 5

http://www.scmfocus.com/demandplanning/2010/09/why-companies- are-selecting-the-wrong-supply-chain-demand-planning-systems/

Chapter 6

http://www.scmfocus.com/productionplanningandscheduling/ 2012/11/16/a-review-of-plan4demands-ppds-webinar/

Chapter 7

http://www.scmfocus.com/enterprisesoftwarepolicy/2012/03/11/ why-the-largest-enterprise-software-companies-have-no-reason-to-innovate/

http://www.scmfocus.com/scmhistory/2010/07/ how-analysts-got-everything-wrong-on-marketplaces/

Chapter 8

http://vimeo.com/14844814

http://blip.tv/scm-focus/google-search-for-misuse-of-inventory-optimization-4122062

http://www.softwaredecisions.org

http://www.scmfocus.com/inventoryoptimizationmultiechelon/2010/01/ its-time-for-the-sap-xapps-program-to-die/

http://www.scmfocus.com/sapprojectmanagement/2012/01/the-end-of-sap-solution-manager/

http://www.scmfocus.com/sapintegration/2011/11/15/what-are-saps-vendor-integration-certifications-worth-on-projects/

Chapter 10

http://www.scmfocus.com/sapplanning/2011/05/19/why-i-no-longer-recommend-using-the-cif/

http://www.softwaredecisions.org

Chapter 11

http://www.softwaredecisions.org

http://www.scmfocus.com/sapprojectmanagement/2011/07/what-is-an-sap-platinum-consultant/

Author Profile

Shaun Snapp is the Founder and Editor of SCM Focus. SCM Focus is one of the largest independent supply chain software analysis and educational sites on the Internet.

After working at several of the largest consulting companies and at i2 Technologies, he became an independent consultant and later started SCM Focus. He maintains a strong interest in comparative software design, and works both in SAP APO, as well as with a variety of best-of-breed supply chain planning vendors. His ongoing relationships with these vendors keep him on the cutting edge of emerging technology.

Primary Sources of Information and Writing Topics

Shaun writes about topics with which he has first-hand experience. These topics range from recovering problematic implementations, to system configuration, to socializing complex software and supply chain concepts in the areas of demand planning, supply planning and production planning.

More broadly, he writes on topics supportive of these applications, which include master data parameter management, integration, analytics, simulation and bill of material management systems. He covers management aspects of enterprise software ranging from software policy to handling consulting partners on SAP projects.

Shaun writes from an implementer's perspective and as a result he focuses on how software is actually used in practice rather than its hypothetical or "pure release note capabilities." Unlike many authors in enterprise software who keep their distance from discussing the realities of software implementation, he writes both on the problems as well as the successes of his software use. This gives him a distinctive voice in the field.

Secondary Sources of Information
In addition to project experience, Shaun's interest in academic literature is a secondary source of information for his books and articles. Intrigued with the historical perspective of supply chain software, much of his writing is influenced by his readings and research into how different categories of supply chain software developed, evolved, and finally became broadly used over time.

Covering the Latest Software Developments
Shaun is focused on supply chain software selections and implementation improvement through writing and consulting, bringing companies some of the newest technologies and methods. Some of the software developments that Shaun showcases at SCM Focus and in books at SCM Focus Press have yet to reach widespread adoption.

Education
Shaun has an undergraduate degree in business from the University of Hawaii, a Masters of Science in Maritime Management from the Maine Maritime Academy and a Masters of Science in Business Logistics from Penn State University. He has taught both logistics and SAP software.

Software Certifications
Shaun has been trained and/or certified in products from i2 Technologies, Servigistics, ToolsGroup and SAP (SD, DP, SNP, SPP, EWM).

Contact
Shaun can be contacted at: shaunsnapp@scmfocus.com or www.scmfocus.com/

Abbreviations

BI—Business Intelligence

CRM—Customer Relationship Management

CSC—Computer Services Corporation

ERP—Enterprise Resource Planning

FTC—Federal Trade Commission

RFP—Request for Proposal

SaaS—Software as a Service

SAP APO—Advanced Planner and Optimizer

SAP BW—Business Warehouse

SAP MDM—Master Data Management

SAP PP/DS—Production Planning and Detailed Scheduling

SAP XI/PI—SAP Process Integration

TCO—Total Cost of Ownership

www.ingramcontent.com/pod-product-compliance
Lightning Source LLC
LaVergne TN
LVHW062317060326
832902LV00013B/2279